HERE AND NOW

Paul Auster is the bestselling author of *Winter Journal*, *Sunset Park*, *Man in the Dark*, *The Brooklyn Follies*, *The Book of Illusions*, *The New York Trilogy*, among many other works. In 2006 he was awarded the Prince of Asturias Prize for Literature and inducted into the American Academy of Arts and Letters. Among his other honours are the Independent Spirit Award for the screenplay of *Smoke* and the Prix Medicis Etranger for *Leviathan*. His work has been translated into more than thirty languages.

J.M. Coetzee's work includes *Waiting for the Barbarians*, *Life & Times of Michael K*, *Boyhood*, *Youth*, *Summertime*, *Disgrace*, *Diary of a Bad Year* and *The Childhood of Jesus*. He has won many literary awards, including the CNA Prize (South Africa's premier literary award), the Prix Etranger Femina, the Jerusalem Prize, and the *Irish Times* International Fiction Prize. He was the first author to win the Booker Prize twice and was awarded the Nobel Prize in Literature in 2003.

9 40255346

PAUL AUSTER and J. M. COETZEE

Here and Now

Letters 2008 – 2011

VINTAGE BOOKS
London

Published by Vintage 2014

4 6 8 10 9 7 5 3

First published in the USA in 2013 by Viking
Penguin Group (USA) Inc., 375 Hudson Street
New York, New York 10014, USA

First published in Great Britain in 2013
by Faber and Faber Ltd
Bloomsbury House
74-77 Great Russell Street
London WC1B 3DA

and

Harvill Secker
Random House, 20 Vauxhall Bridge Road,
London SW1V 2SA

www.vintage-books.co.uk

Addresses for companies within The Random House Group Limited
can be found at: www.randomhouse.co.uk/offices.htm

The Random House Group Limited Reg. No. 954009

A CIP catalogue record for this book
is available from the British Library

ISBN 9780099584223

The Random House Group Limited supports the Forest Stewardship
Council® (FSC®), the leading international forest-certification
organisation. Our books carrying the FSC label are printed on FSC®-
certified paper. FSC is the only forest-certification scheme supported
by the leading environmental organisations, including Greenpeace.
Our paper procurement policy can be found at:
www.randomhouse.co.uk/environment

Printed and bound by Clays Ltd, St Ives plc

HERE AND NOW

Dear Paul,

I have been thinking about friendships, how they arise, why they last—some of them—so long, longer than the passional attachments of which they are sometimes (wrongly) considered to be pale imitations. I was about to write a letter to you about all of this, starting with the observation that, considering how important friendships are in social life, and how much they mean to us, particularly during childhood, it is surprising how little has been written on the subject.

But then I asked myself whether this was really true. So before I sat down to write I went off to the library to do a quick check. And, lo and behold, I could not have been more wrong. The library catalog listed whole books on the subject, scores of books, many of them quite recent. But when I took a step further and actually had a look at these books, I recovered my self-respect somewhat. I had been right, or half-right, after all: what the books had to say about friendship was of little interest, most of it. Friendship, it would seem, remains a bit of a riddle: we know it is important, but as to why people become friends and remain friends we can only guess.

(What do I mean when I say that what is written is of little interest? Compare friendship with love. There are hundreds of interesting things to say about love. For instance: Men fall in love with women who remind them of their mothers, or rather, who both remind them and don't remind them of their mothers, who are and are not their mothers at the same time. True? Maybe, maybe not. Interesting? Definitely. Now turn to friendship. Whom do men choose as friends? Other men of roughly the same age, with similar interests, say the books. True? Maybe. Interesting? Definitely not.)

Let me list the few observations on friendship, culled from my visits to the library, that I found of actual interest.

Item. One cannot be friends with an inanimate object, says Aristotle (*Ethics*, chapter 8). Of course not! Who ever said one could? But interesting nevertheless: all of a sudden one sees where modern linguistic philosophy got its inspiration. Two thousand four hundred years ago Aristotle was demonstrating that what looked like philosophical postulates could be no more than rules of grammar. In the sentence "I am friends with X," he says, X has to be an animate noun.

Item. One can have friends without wanting to see them, says Charles Lamb. True; and interesting too—another way in which amical feelings are unlike erotic attachments.

Item. Friends, or at least male friends in the West, don't talk about how they feel toward each other. Compare the garrulity of lovers. Thus far, not very interesting. Yet when the friend dies, what outpourings of grief: "Alas, too late!" (Montaigne on La Boétie, Milton on Edward King). (Question: Is love garrulous because desire is by nature ambivalent—Shakespeare, *Sonnets*—while friendship is taciturn because it is straightforward, without ambivalence?)

Finally, a remark by Christopher Tietjens in Ford Madox Ford's *Parade's End*: that one goes to bed with a woman in order to be able to talk to her. Implication: that turning a woman into a mistress is only a first step; the second step, turning her into a friend, is the one that matters; but being friends with a woman you haven't slept with is in practice impossible because there is too much unspoken in the air.

If it is indeed so hard to say anything of interest about friendship, then a further insight becomes possible: that, unlike love or politics, which are never what they seem to be, friendship is what it seems to be. Friendship is transparent.

The most interesting reflections on friendship come from the ancient world. Why so? Because in ancient times people did not regard the philosophical stance as an inherently skeptical one, therefore did not take it as given that friendship must be other than it seems to be, or conversely conclude that if friendship is what it seems to be, then it cannot be a fit subject for philosophy.

All good wishes,

John

Dear John,

This is a question I have given much thought to over the years. I can't say I have developed any coherent position about friendship, but in response to your letter (which unleashed a whirlwind of thoughts and memories in me), perhaps this is the moment to try.

To begin with, I will confine myself to male friendship, friendship between men, friendship between boys.

1) Yes, there are friendships that are transparent and unambivalent (to use your terms), but in my experience not many of them. This might have something to do with another one of the terms you use: taciturn. You are correct to say that male friends (at least in the West) tend not to "talk about how they feel toward each other." I would take this one step further and add: men tend not to talk about how they feel, period. And if you don't know how your friend feels, or what he feels, or why he feels, can you honestly say that you know your friend? And yet friendships endure, often for many decades, in this ambiguous zone of not-knowing.

At least three of my novels deal directly with male friendship, are in a sense stories *about* male friendship—*The Locked Room*, *Leviathan*, and *Oracle Night*—and in each case, this no-man's land of not-knowing that stands between friends becomes the stage on which the dramas are played out.

An example from life. For the past twenty-five years, one of my closest friends—perhaps the closest male friend of my adulthood—is one of the least garrulous people I have ever known. He is older than I am (by eleven years), but there is much we have in common: both writers, both idiotically obsessed with sports, both with long marriages to remarkable women, and, most important and most difficult to define, a certain unarticulated but shared feeling about how one is supposed to live—an ethics of manhood. And yet, much as I care for this person, willing as I would be to rip the shirt off my back for him in time of trouble, our conversations are almost without exception bland and insipid, utterly banal. We communicate by emitting short grunts, reverting to a kind of shorthand language that would be incomprehensible to a stranger. As for our work (the driving force of both our lives), we rarely even mention it.

To demonstrate how closely this man plays his cards to his vest, one small anecdote. A number of years ago, a new novel of his was about to appear in galleys. I told him how much I was looking forward to reading it (sometimes we send each other finished manuscripts, sometimes we wait for the galleys), and he said that I should be receiving a copy quite soon. The galleys arrived in the mail the following week, I opened the package, flipped through the book, and discovered that it was dedicated to me. I was touched, of course, deeply moved in fact—but the point is that my friend never said a word about it. Not the smallest hint, not the tiniest anticipatory wink, nothing.

What am I trying to say? That I know this man and don't know him. That he is my friend, my dearest friend, in spite of this not-knowing. If he went out and robbed a bank tomorrow, I would be shocked. On the other hand, if I learned that he was cheating on his wife, that he had a young mistress stashed away in an apartment somewhere, I would be disappointed, but I wouldn't be shocked. Anything is possible, and men do keep secrets, even from their closest friends. In the event of my friend's marital infidelity, I would feel disappointed (because he had let down his wife, someone I am very fond of), but I would also feel hurt (because he hadn't confided in me, which would mean our friendship wasn't as close as I thought it was).

(A sudden brain wave. The best and most lasting friendships are based on admiration. This is the bedrock feeling that connects two people over the long term. You admire someone for what he does, for what he is, for how he negotiates his path through the world. Your admiration enhances him in your eyes, ennobles him, elevates him to a status you believe is above your own. And if that person admires you as well—and therefore enhances you, ennobles you, elevates you to a status he believes is above his own—then you are in a position of absolute equality. You are both giving more than you receive, both receiving more than you give, and in the reciprocity of this exchange, friendship blooms. From Joubert's *Notebooks* (1809): "He must not only cultivate his friends, but cultivate his friendships within himself. They must be kept, cared for, watered." And again Joubert: "We always lose the friendship of those who lose our esteem.")

2) Boys. Childhood is the most intense period of our lives because most of what we do then we are doing for the first time. I have little to offer here but a memory, but that memory seems to underscore the infinite value we place on friendship when we are young, even very young. I was five years old. Billy, my first friend, entered my life in ways that elude me now. I remember him as an odd and jovial character with strong opinions and a highly developed talent for mischief (some-

Paul Auster and J. M. Coetzee

thing I lacked to an appalling degree). He had a severe speech impediment, and when he talked his words were so garbled, so clogged with the saliva buildup in his mouth, that no one could understand what he said—except little Paul, who acted as his interpreter. Much of our time together was spent roaming around our New Jersey suburban neighborhood looking for small dead animals—mostly birds, but an occasional frog or chipmunk—and burying the corpses in the flower bed along the side of my house. Solemn rituals, handmade wooden crosses, no laughing allowed. Billy detested girls, refusing to fill in the pages of our coloring books that showed representations of female figures, and because his favorite color was green, he was convinced that the blood running through his teddy bear's veins was green. *Ecce* Billy. Then, when we were six and a half or seven, he and his family moved to another town. Heartbreak, followed by weeks if not months of longing for my absent friend. At last, my mother relented and gave me permission to make the expensive telephone call to Billy's new house. The content of our conversation has been blotted from my mind, but I remember my feelings as vividly as I remember what I had for breakfast this morning. I felt what I would later feel as an adolescent when talking on the phone to the girl I had fallen in love with.

You make a distinction in your letter between friendship and love. When we are very small, before our erotic lives begin, there is no distinction. Friendship and love are one.

3) Friendship and love are not one. Men and women. The difference between marriage and friendship. A last quotation from Joubert (1801): "Do not choose for your wife any woman you would not choose as your friend if she were a man."

A rather absurd formulation, I suppose (how can a woman be a man?), but one gets the point, and in essence it is not far from your remark about *Parade's End* by Ford Madox Ford and the funny, whimsical assertion that "one goes to bed with a woman in order to be able to talk to her."

Marriage is above all a conversation, and if husband and wife do not figure out a way to become friends, the marriage has little chance of surviving. Friendship is a component of marriage, but marriage is an ever-evolving free-for-all, a continual work in progress, a constant demand to reach down into one's depths and reinvent oneself in relation to the other, whereas friendship pure and simple (that is, friendship outside marriage), tends to be more static, more polite, more superficial. We crave friendships because we are social beings, born from other beings and destined to live among other beings until the day we die, and yet think of the quarrels that sometimes erupt in even the best marriages, the passionate disagreements, the hot-headed insults, the slammed doors and broken crockery, and one quickly understands that such behavior would not be countenanced within the decorous rooms of friendship. Friendship is good manners, kindness, steadiness of affect. Friends who shout at each other rarely remain friends. Husbands and wives who shout at each other usually stay married—often happily married.

Can men and women be friends? I think so. As long as there is no physical attraction on either side. Once sex enters the equation, all bets are off.

4) To be continued. But other aspects of friendship need to be discussed as well: a) Friendships that wither and die; b) Friendships between people who do not necessarily share

common interests (work friendships, school friendships, war friendships); c) The concentric circles of friendship: the core intimates, the less intimate but much liked ones, the ones who live far away, the pleasant acquaintances, and so on; d) All the other points in your letter I haven't addressed.

With warmest thoughts from hot New York,

Paul

September 12, 2008

Dear Paul,

A response to your letter of July 29—sorry to have taken so long.

Dorothy has been away in Europe (Sweden, the UK) attending academic conferences. The latter part of the trip has been a bit of a nightmare—she developed bronchitis and had to cancel travel plans within the UK, then yesterday had a fall which is making it hard for her to move around. She is due back in Australia next week.

The good news is that she will be accompanying me to Estoril [Portugal]. We are both looking forward to that, and to seeing you and Siri again.

All good wishes,

John

Paul Auster and J. M. Coetzee

September 11, 2008

Dear Paul,

"The best and most lasting friendships are based on admiration," you write.

I would be cautious about accepting this as a general law—it seems to me less true for women than for men—but I do agree with the sentiment behind it. Plato writes of our desire to be held in honor by our peers as a spur to excellence. In an age still dominated by Darwin, Nietzsche, and Freud, there is a tendency to reduce the desire to be held in honor to something less idealistic—a will to power, for instance, or a drive to spread one's genes. But identifying the desire to be held in esteem as one of the primary forces in the soul yields valuable insights, it seems to me. For instance, it suggests why athletic sports—activities with no parallel in the rest of creation—are so important to human beings, men in particular. Men run faster or kick the ball farther not in the hope that pretty girls with good genes will want to mate with them but in the hope that their peers, other men with whom they feel bonded in mutual admiration, will admire them. Much the same holds, mutatis mutandis, in other fields of endeavor.

I agree too that it is hard to continue to regard someone as a friend once he/she has dishonored him/herself in one's eyes. Perhaps this helps to explain why codes of honor are kept alive among otherwise amoral criminal bands: the band can hold together only as long as members adhere to the code and do not fall into dishonor in each other's eyes.

You write about childhood friendships. It has struck me recently how free we feel as parents, particularly as parents of young children, to let our children know how we feel about their friends—whether we approve of a new friend or see the friend as "bad company." If I had my life as a parent to live again, I would be more circumspect about this. It's unfair to a child to make him/her try to guess what it is about the new friend that makes the friend unattractive to the parent. Much of the time, what makes the friend unappealing is entirely outside the child's radar: class snobbery, for instance, or some story going the rounds about the friend's parents. Sometimes the very quality that makes the new friend alluring—greater savvy about sexual matters, for instance—is what puts the parent off.

As for friendships between men and women, it does strike me as curious that the usual order of events nowadays is for a man and a woman first to become lovers and then later friends, rather than first friends and later lovers. If this generalization is true, are we to think of friendship between a man and a woman as in some sense higher than erotic love, a stage to which they may graduate after mere sexual experience of each other? There are certainly people who think this way: the course of erotic love is unpredictable, they say, it does not endure, it can turn unexpectedly into its opposite; whereas friendship is constant and enduring, can spur the friends to become better people (as you have described).

I think we should be suspicious of accepting too readily this claim, and the consequences that flow from it. For instance, it is conventional wisdom that it is unwise for a man and a woman who have long been friends ("mere" friends) to take the step into physical love. Sleeping with a friend is a tame experience, says conventional wisdom; a good friend does not have the element of mystery that eros demands. Is this in fact true? Surely the allure of incest between brother and sister is precisely that of stepping from the all too well known into the mysterious unknown.

Incest used to be a big topic in literature (Musil, Nabokov) but no longer seems to be. I wonder why. Perhaps because the notion of sex as a quasi-religious experience—and therefore of incest as a challenge to the gods—has evaporated into thin air.

Best wishes,

John

Dear John,

Please tell Dorothy to be more careful. Bronchitis is bad enough, but falling down is terrible. I trust (hope) that no bones were broken. Siri and I are extremely happy that she will be going to Portugal in November.

I have been traveling—and am about to take off again in a couple of days. No time right now to give a full response, but I promise to send one as soon as I return in mid-October.

Curious that you should have mentioned brother-sister incest in your letter. Such a thing happens in my new book (and is dwelled upon at some length)—and indeed, the sex is a quasi-religious experience for the two characters (to use your words). Does that mean I am hopelessly out of date? Probably.

As for admiration, I was referring to friendships between men. But more about that after I return . . .

      With a handshake,

      Paul

Dear John,

I wanted to write sooner but returned to New York suffering from a bad intestinal bug that has kept me on my back until this morning. Fortunately, I managed to get through seventeen days of hectic travels in one piece and became ill only on the final night, after the last of my chores was done. A predictable result, no doubt. You live on pure adrenaline and then, once the adrenaline ebbs out of you, you understand that you've pushed yourself too hard. I look forward to Portugal as a respite, a period of calm and composure, the next best thing to a holiday.

In your last letter, you mentioned "athletic sports—activities with no parallel in the rest of creation . . . ," which reminded me of some brief exchanges about sports while we were driving around France last summer. Would it interest you to delve into this matter? I have read your "[Four] Notes on Rugby" from thirty years ago. Provocative and tightly argued, but if you care to revisit this territory, I would be happy to go there with you. (My own little contribution to the subject is "The Best Substitute for War" in *Collected Prose*, a commission from the *New York Times Magazine* for an issue about the millennium a decade ago. My assignment: Write—very briefly—about the best game of the past thousand years. I chose soccer.)

Possible points to discuss: 1) Sports and aggression; 2) Playing a sport as opposed to watching others play it; 3) The phenomenology—and mysteries—of fandom; 4) Individual sports (tennis, golf, swimming, archery, boxing, track-and-field) as opposed to team sports; 5) The slow and ineluctable decline of boxing. Parallel phenomenon: the universal indifference to track-and-field records. Forty, fifty years ago, the whole world waited eagerly for the first seven-foot high jump, the first sixteen-foot pole vault, the newest sub-four-minute mile. Why the lack of interest now?; 6) Sport as drama, narrative, suspense; 7) Sports ruled by the clock (football, basketball, rugby) as opposed to sports with no time limits (baseball, cricket); 8) Sports and commerce; 9) Sports and nationalism; 10) *Homo ludens.*

With all good thoughts,

Paul

Paul Auster and J. M. Coetzee

Dear Siri,*

How are you? I am only just recovering from the flu that hit the judging panel in Portugal. It's been a miserable time. I hope you escaped.

I needn't tell you how much fun it was to have all that time to spend with you and Paul.

I'm appending a letter which contains the blinding insight I promised you and Paul during our last days in Cascais. Could I ask you to print it out and pass it on to Paul? I thoroughly approve of old-fashioned letters with stamps on them, but in this case I feel I have been out of action so long that I need to harness the energy of the Internet.

Love,

John

---

* e-mail to Siri Hustvedt (Auster's wife)

LETTER TO P. A.

Dear Paul,

Toward the end of 2008, something happened in the realm of high finance as a result of which, we are informed, most of us are now poorer (poorer in money terms, that is to say) than a few months ago. What exactly it was that happened has not been fully spelled out and is perhaps not known precisely: it is a subject of excited discussion among experts. But no one questions that something happened.

The question is, what is the something that happened? Was it something real, or was it one of those imaginary somethings that have real consequences, like the apparition of the Virgin that turned Lourdes into a flourishing tourist center?

Let me list some real events as a result of which we—as a nation, as a society, not just as scattered individuals here and there—might wake up one day suddenly poorer.

A plague of locusts could devour our crops.

There could be drought, lasting year after year.

A murrain could devastate our herds and flocks.

An earthquake could destroy roads and bridges and factories and homes.

Our country could be invaded by a foreign army, which would pillage our cities, capture our treasure-hoards, cart away our food stores, and turn us into slaves.

We could be drawn into an unending foreign war, to which we would have to send thousands of strong young men while we poured our remaining resources into the purchase of armaments.

A foreign navy could take over mastery of the seas, preventing our colonies from sending us shiploads of food and consignments of precious metals.

By the grace of God, no such calamities befell us in 2008. Our cities stand intact, our farms remain productive, our shops are full of goods.

What then happened to make us poorer?

The answer we are given is that certain numbers changed. Certain numbers that used to be high suddenly became low, and as a result we are poorer.

But the numbers 0, 1, 2, . . . 9 are mere signs, no less than the letters a, b, c, . . . z are mere signs. So it could not have been the drop in the numbers that in itself made us poorer. It must have been something that was signified by the drop in the numbers that did it.

But what exactly was it, signified by the new, lower numbers, that made us poorer? The answer is: another set of numbers. The culpable numbers stood for other numbers, and those other numbers stood for yet other numbers, and so on.

Where does this regression in sets of signifiers end? Where is the thing itself that they signify: the plague of locusts or the foreign invasion? Nowhere that I can see. The world is as it was before. Nothing has changed except for the numbers.

If nothing has really happened, if the numbers reflect no reality but on the contrary simply refer to other numbers, why, I ask, do we have to accept the verdict that we are now poorer and must start behaving as if we are poorer? Why not, I ask, simply throw away this particular set of numbers, numbers that make us unhappy and don't reflect a reality anyway, and make up new numbers for ourselves, perhaps numbers that show us to be richer than we used to be, though it might be better to make up numbers that show us exactly as we are, with our well-stocked larders and our tight roofs and our hinterland full of productive factories and farms?

The response I receive to this proposal (this "naive" proposal) is a pitying head shake. The numbers that confront us, the numbers we have inherited, I am told, do indeed describe the way things are; the internal logic in the progression of those numbers from higher to lower, from early 2008 to late 2008, describes a real impoverishment that has taken place.

So we have a standoff. On the one hand, people like myself who don't believe anything real has taken place and demand ostensive proof that it has. On the other hand, those in the know, whose line is: "You plainly don't understand how the system works."

In Book 7 of *The Republic* Plato asks us to imagine a society in which people spend their waking hours sitting in rows inside a dark cave, staring at screens on which various flickerings are taking place. None of them have ever been outside the cave, none of them are acquainted with anything beyond the flickerings on their screens. All accept without question that what they see on the screens is all there is to see.

One day one of these people happens to get up and stagger outdoors. His eyes, unused to the light, are blinded, but he does catch glimpses of trees, flowers, and a multiplicity of other forms that do not in the slightest resemble the flickerings he is used to.

Shielding his eyes, he returns to his fellows. This place where we live is actually a cave, he says, and the cave has an outside, and outside the cave it is quite different from inside. There is real life going on out there.

His fellows snigger. You poor fool, they say, don't you recognize a dream when you see one? This is what is real (they gesture toward the screens).

It is all there in Plato (427–348 BCE), down to the details of the hunched shoulders, the flickering screens, and the myopia.

All the best,

John

P.S.: I am not unaware that in proposing that we make up a new, "good" set of numbers to take the place of the old, "bad" numbers and install these new numbers in all the world's computers, I am proposing no less than the discarding of the old, bad economic system and its replacement by a new, good one—in other words, the inauguration of universal economic justice. This is a project which our present leaders have neither the aptitude nor the will nor indeed the desire to carry out.

December 9, 2008

Dear John,

Your "Letter to P. A." has turned up in Siri's computer, and she has just printed it out for me. I don't know when it was written or sent, and if I am days or weeks late in answering, please forgive me.

Before addressing Plato's cave and the utter collapse of civilization as we know it, I want to tell you and Dorothy what an immense pleasure it was spending those days in Portugal with you. The sun, the conversations, the meals, the unhurried pace of things—all memorable. Yes, we had to sit through some dreadful films, but the chance to see one brilliant film was adequate compensation for our suffering.

LETTER TO J. C.

What we are talking about here, I think, is the power of fiction to affect reality, and the supreme fiction of our world is money. What is money but worthless pieces of paper? If that paper has acquired value, it is only because large numbers of people have chosen to give it value. The system runs on faith. Not truth or reality, but collective belief.

The numbers you refer to are born out of this belief. The numbers represent the paper, and in major financial transactions (stock trading and banking as opposed, say, to buying groceries), the paper has disappeared and been converted into numbers. Numbers talk to numbers, and we are thrust into a realm of pure abstraction. That is why your allusion to Plato's cave is apt. The numbers are the shadows flickering on the wall. Or, as Siri's father used to say: There are two kinds of people in the world. The people who work for their money, and the people whose money works for them.

Now we have entered a period in which the numbers have begun to frighten us. I agree with you that the crisis seems unreal, unmoored to any concrete facts. Banks collapsing because of foolish, risky investments in the future cost of mortgages (numbers talking to numbers), multi-billion-dollar bailouts, and suddenly faith in the system (the collective belief in the fiction we have created) is faltering. Yesterday, calm; today, widespread panic.

Unfortunately, this panic, which is no more or less grounded in reality than yesterday's calm, is producing tangible results— the equivalent of your plague of locusts, your pestilence.

I am referring to the so-called credit crisis. Banks have become too afraid to lend anyone money. Let's imagine you are the owner of a small factory that produces armchairs. You need to acquire new equipment to keep your business running, and because you don't have enough cash on hand to pay for it, you go to a bank to ask for a loan. The bank turns you down, and because your business cannot survive without the new equipment, you are forced to fire half your workers, to declare bankruptcy, to shut your doors for good.

Last month alone, more than half a million workers in America lost their jobs. The panic has led to an ever-expanding unemployment problem, and people without work are indeed poor—in spite of a general sense, as you put it, that our larders are well stocked.

The crisis will end only when the panic ends. But what will cause the panic to end is a mystery to me.

Your idea of making up a new set of numbers might be a

beginning. Another solution, which occurred to me the other day, would be for governments to start printing vast amounts of money and distribute tens of thousands of dollars to every person in the world. There must be a flaw in my thinking (am I overlooking the possibility of rampant inflation?), but, if I'm not mistaken, the bailouts are being funded in precisely this way: by printing more money.

All best,

Paul

Paul Auster and J. M. Coetzee

Dear John,

Only yesterday, a week after it was sent, the cover note accompanying your "Letter to P. A." surfaced in Siri's computer. Somehow, she had managed to miss it (we are a hopeless pair when it comes to the digital life), and I was happy to learn that you enjoyed Portugal as much as I did and sorry to hear about your flu. (I had a nasty one earlier in the fall and know how wretched those microbes can be.) I trust you are back in form now. The knife-like precision of your letter could not have been achieved by an ill man.

Your reference to the film festival reminded me of a curious story I would like to share with you. It dates back to 1997, when I was a member of the jury at Cannes. It happened to be the fiftieth anniversary of the festival, and the organizers decided to gather together as many prize winners from the past as possible and have them sit for a large group photograph. For some reason, jury members were asked to participate as well—which was how I wound up in that picture of more than a hundred people.

I am looking at the photo now, and among the directors I recognize are Antonioni, Almodóvar, Wadja, John Boorman, David Lynch, Tim Burton, Jane Campion, Altman, Wenders, Polanski, Coppola, the Coen brothers, Mike Leigh, Bertolucci, and Scorsese. The actors include Gina Lollobrigida (!), Lauren Bacall, Johnny Depp, Vittorio Gassman, Claudia Cardinale, Liv Ullmann, Charlotte Rampling, Bibi Andersson, Vanessa Redgrave, Irène Jacob, Helen Mirren, Jeanne Moreau, and Anjelica Huston.

Before we took our places for the photo, there was a cocktail reception that lasted for about an hour. I'm not sure I have ever stood in a room more charged with human electricity. It felt as if everyone there wanted to meet and talk to everyone else, that the excitement generated by such a gathering had turned these stars and legends into a mass of hyperactive schoolchildren.

I was introduced to a number of people, had short conversations with some of them, and then, in the swirling mayhem, found myself shaking the hand of Charlton Heston. Of all the people in that room, he was the one I was least interested in talking to. Not only did I think he was a bad actor (stiff, unconvincing, pompous), but I found his politics abhorrent. You probably know about his involvement with the National Rifle Association and his putrid right-wing pronouncements, which always seemed to get a lot of attention from the American press. But what could I do? It was neither the time nor the place to challenge him, and before long I realized I was trapped. Heston had no idea who I was, of course, but he, too, infected by the electricity in the room, was in high spirits, and he appeared to enjoy talking to me. He talked, and I listened, and for the next ten or fifteen minutes he reminisced about his earlier visits to Cannes, his long career in the movies, how wonderful he thought this gathering was, and how humbled he felt in the presence of all these remarkably talented people. In spite of my prejudice against him, I had to admit that in some ways he was a "perfectly nice guy."

The festival ended a few days later, and I went home to New York. Two or three days after that, I went to Chicago. I had promised my American publisher to attend the annual

Book Expo event in order to give a reading from a book of mine that was due to come out in the fall. I arrived on a Saturday. After checking into my hotel, I took a cab to the McCormick Center—which is an enormous place, I discovered, probably the size of fifty airplane hangars, and every inch of the floor was crammed with publishers' booths, hundreds and hundreds of booths, perhaps thousands. By the time I found my way to the Henry Holt stand, my bladder was nearly bursting. Someone pointed me in the direction of the men's room (about a mile and a half away), and off I went, walking briskly down one aisle after another, passing scores of publishers' booths in the process, and just as I was approaching my destination, I glanced to my right, and there, sitting at a table signing books, was Charlton Heston, the same Charlton Heston I had met in Cannes a week earlier. The banner above him read: National Rifle Association. Needless to say, I didn't stop to exchange pleasantries. The "perfectly nice guy" was back in his element, and I had no desire to talk to him. Nevertheless, I felt rattled. What were the odds, I wondered, of meeting a man at a French film festival, and then, just days later, running into him again at a book fair in Chicago?

I did my reading and flew home the next morning, Sunday. The following day, Monday, I was scheduled to have lunch in Manhattan with the French actress Juliette Binoche, who was considering whether to accept a role in the film I was preparing, *Lulu on the Bridge*. (That is another story—and far too complicated to go into here.) I arrived at her hotel a little past noon—a small, elegant, very expensive place on Madison Avenue called The Mark. I announced myself at the front desk and then ambled around the lobby as I waited for J.B. to come downstairs. No one else was there. Except for the clerk behind the desk and myself, the lobby was deserted. After a minute or so, the elevator door opened, and out stepped a man: a large old man, somewhat bent over, who walked with slow, shuffling steps. He began moving in my direction, and an instant later I realized that I was looking at . . . Charlton Heston.

He glanced up, took note of my presence, and stopped. Recognition flickered in his eyes. Wagging his finger at me and beginning to smile, he said: "I know you from somewhere, don't I?"

"We met at Cannes last week," I said. "We talked for a little while before the group photo session."

"Ah, of course," he said, smiling in earnest now and reaching out to shake my hand. "So good to see you again."

I didn't bother to mention Chicago.

He asked me how I was doing. Fine, I said, just fine. And you? I asked, how have you been doing? Fine, he said, just fine, and then he shuffled on past and went outside through the revolving door.

What am I to make of this, John? Do things like this happen to you, or am I the only one?

Paul

December 30, 2008

Dear Siri,*

I have two questions (two favors) to ask, the first to/of you, the second to/of Paul. Would you mind passing the second on?

(1) I have engaged to write a review of a new edition of Samuel Beckett's letters of the years 1929–1940. In the mid-1930s Beckett was in therapy with Wilfred Bion. Am I correct in thinking you know more than a little about Bion? Is there a good book or article that I can read to get an idea of Bion's approach to therapy?

(2) The edition in question appears to be based on a sharp distinction between Beckett's literary correspondence and his personal correspondence. None of the latter is included. The editors also seem determined not to say anything about Beckett's private life. One consequence is that the reader of the letters has little idea of why Beckett keeps shuttling between Dublin and Paris and Hamburg and London (mostly, one suspects, eros is the spur).

The editors also express their gratitude lavishly to Beckett's nephew and the Beckett Estate.

My question is: Do you have any experience of Edward Beckett? Is there an identifiable agenda behind the way he controls the Beckett corpus?

All the best,

John

* e-mail to Siri Hustvedt

Dear Paul,

The "crisis in world finance" that I wrote about last time seems set to continue into the new year. At this point I think I should quit my role as commentator on economic affairs. I am reminded of Ezra Pound, whose unhingement began during the depression of the 1930s, when he convinced himself he was seeing things about how the economy worked that other people, wrapped up in fictions, were too blind to see: in short order he turned himself into what Gertrude Stein called "a village explainer," Uncle Ez.

It is high summer in this hemisphere, and I spent most of Sunday sitting in front of a television screen (shades of Wall Street!) watching the third day of a five-day game of cricket between the national teams of Australia and South Africa. I was absorbed, I was emotionally involved, I tore myself away only reluctantly. In order to watch the game I put aside the two or three books I am in the middle of reading.

Cricket has been played for centuries. As with all games, there are only so many moves you can make, only so many effects you can cause. It is very likely that the proceedings in Melbourne on Sunday, December 28, 2008, duplicate in every respect that counts the proceedings of some other day's cricket in some other place. By the age of thirty, any serious spectator must have moments of déjà vu—more than moments, extended periods. And justifiably so: it's all been done before. Whereas one thing you can say about a good book is that it has never been written before.

So why waste my time slumped in front of a television

screen watching young men at play? For, I concede, it _is_ a waste of time. I have an experience (a secondhand experience), but it does me no good that I can detect. I learn nothing. I come away with nothing.

Does any of this sound familiar to you? Does it strike a chord you recognize? Is sport simply like sin: one disapproves of it but one yields because the flesh is weak?

Yours ever,

John

Dear John,

Siri will be writing to you separately about Bion . . . but as for Beckett's nephew, I'm afraid I've had no direct contact with him. When I was preparing the Centenary Edition [of S.B.'s work] a few years ago, however, I was told by the editor at Grove Press that Edward was very pleased with the project and gave it his wholehearted endorsement. If you would like to be in touch with him yourself, I could easily arrange it for you through my British publisher, Faber & Faber. As you know, they have had the rights to Beckett's plays for years, but recently, through the efforts of Stephen Page, the young head man there, they have bought out John Calder and now own the rights to all of Beckett's prose as well. Edward surely must have been involved in those negotiations.

As far as I can tell, Edward's somewhat crotchety behavior over the years concerning permissions to perform or publish his uncle's works is an effort to respect S.B.'s wishes, to imagine how the somewhat crotchety S.B. would have acted in each instance were he still alive. But this distinction between literary and personal correspondence makes no sense to me. Years ago, I was contacted by one of the editors of S.B.'s letters (a professor at Emory University, if I'm not mistaken) and sent her photocopies of all the notes and letters I had received from Beckett. According to her, they were aiming to publish a complete correspondence and were hunkering down for what they were certain would be many years of work. At long last, it seems, the first volume is finished.

Who is the publisher—and who are you writing the review for?

Concerning Beckett's travels, I'm not sure that love was the motivating factor. Knowlson's biography is a good source of information on these comings and goings. Many of the events are dim to me now, but I believe that Beckett first went to Paris on a teaching fellowship after graduating from Trinity. He was there for a year or two, then returned to Dublin, where he taught for a while and started cracking up. His principal reason for going to London was to receive treatment from Bion (I think). The trips to Germany were mostly about looking at art. The only woman he knew there was someone named Peggy Sinclair (the daughter of a relative by marriage, his first flame—who died young of TB).

I'm afraid that none of this will be of much help to you, but you might dip into the Knowlson to see if the facts tally with my memories. If I'm not mistaken, he discusses Bion at some length.

Happy new year to you and Dorothy!

Paul

Dear Paul,

Thanks for correcting me on Beckett's nephew. It seemed to me that the editors of the new *Letters* were drawing rather too sharp a line between the literary and the personal, and I surmised—erroneously—that the estate might be behind it.

The publisher is Cambridge. My review will be in the *NY Review of Books*.

On Charlton Heston: It doesn't seem to me strange that, operating in a film environment, you should keep running into another person from that environment. What is bizarre is that it should be Charlton Heston. It begins to sound like one of the dreams from Freud's dream book.

All good wishes,

John

Dear John,

Your snappy, witty letter from 12/30 arrived just two hours before I left for the airport. Now I am in Europe again, a frigid Paris, twelve noon exactly, sitting in my hotel room, unable to go on with the nap I was hoping to take to ward off the effects of a sleepless night. Excuse the funny stationery, excuse the crappy ballpoint pen. For some reason, Paris hotel rooms are not equipped with typewriters.

I'm more than happy to leave behind our ruminations on economics. It is a subject I am ill qualified to talk about. Needless to say, I am an ardent believer in universal happiness. I would like everyone in the world to have satisfying, fulfilling work, for everyone to earn enough to escape the menace of poverty, but I have no idea how to achieve such worthy goals. Therefore, I will pass over these matters in silence.

Some last words on the Charlton Heston saga. You argue that those chance meetings became possible because we were both moving in a film milieu, traveling in the same circle. But the fact is that only the first meeting had anything to do with film. The second took place at a book fair in Chicago, the third in a New York hotel lobby. Hence my confusion and amazement, my feeling that those encounters were utterly implausible—as if they were events (as you suggest) not from real life but from a dream.

Last week, I reread *Crime and Punishment* for the third or fourth time. I was suddenly struck by plot manipulations that resembled the Charlton Heston story. The most unlikely people wind up living next door to one another. Dunya's fiancé *just happens* to be in the same building as Sonya's stepmother. The man who nearly ruined her (Dunya) *just happens* to be living in the apartment next to Sonya's. Implausible? Yes, but highly effective in creating the atmosphere of a fever dream, which gives the book its tremendous force. What I am saying, I suppose, is that there are things that happen to us in the real world that resemble fiction. And if fiction turns out to be real, then perhaps we have to rethink our definition of reality . . .

WATCHING SPORTS ON T.V.

I agree with you that it is a useless activity, an utter waste of time. And yet how many hours of my life have I wasted in precisely this way, how many afternoons have I squandered just as you did on December 28th? The total count is no doubt appalling, and merely to think about it fills me with embarrassment.

You talk about sin (jokingly), but perhaps the real term is *guilty pleasure*, or perhaps just *pleasure*. In my own case, the sports I am interested in and watch regularly are the ones I played as a boy. One knows and understands the game intimately, and therefore one can appreciate the prowess, the often dazzling skills, of professionals. I don't care a lick about ice hockey, for example—because I never played it and don't truly understand it. Also, in my own case, I tend to focus on and follow specific teams. One's involvement becomes deeper when each player is a familiar figure, a known quantity, and this familiarity *increases one's capacity to endure boredom*, all those dreary moments when nothing much of anything is happening.

There is no question that games have a strong narrative component. We follow the twists and turns of the combat in order to learn the final outcome. But no, it is not quite like reading a book—at least not the kinds of books you and I try to write. But perhaps it's more closely related to genre literature. Think of thrillers or detective novels, for example . . .

[Just now, an unexpected call from a friend, who is waiting downstairs. I have to go, but will continue when I return.] *3 hours later:*

. . . which are always the same book, endlessly repeated, thousands of subtle variations on the same story, and nevertheless the public has an insatiable hunger for these novels. As if each one were the reenactment of a ritual.

The narrative aspect, yes, which keeps us watching until the final play, the final tick of the clock, but all in all I tend to think of sports as a kind of performance art. You complain about the déjà vu quality of so many games and matches. But doesn't the same thing happen when you go to a recital of your favorite Beethoven piano sonata? You already know the piece by heart, but you want to hear how this particular pianist will interpret it. There are pedestrian pianists and athletes, and then someone comes along who takes your breath away.

I wonder if any two contests have ever been *exactly* alike, play for play. Perhaps. All snowflakes look the same, but common wisdom says that each one is unique. More than six billion people inhabit this planet, and supposedly everyone's fingerprints are different from anyone else's. Of the many hundreds of baseball games I have watched—perhaps even thousands—nearly every one has had some small detail or event I have never seen in any other game.

There is pleasure in the new, but also pleasure in the known. The pleasure of eating food one likes, the pleasure of sex. No matter how exotic or complex one's erotic life might be, an orgasm is an orgasm, and we anticipate them with pleasure because of the pleasure they have given us in the past.

Still, one does feel rather stupid after spending an entire day in front of a television set watching young men hurl their bodies against one another. The books sit on the table unread. You don't know where the hours have gone, and, even worse, your team has lost. So I say from Paris, knowing that when the New York football Giants play a crucial playoff game against a tough Philadelphia team tomorrow, I won't be able to watch—and I am filled with regret.

With a big salute across oceans and continents,

Paul

Dear Paul,

You seem to treat sport as a mainly aesthetic affair, and the pleasures of sports spectatorship as mainly aesthetic pleasures. I am dubious about this approach, and for a number of reasons. Why is football big business, while ballet—whose aesthetic attractions are surely superior—has to be subsidized? Why is a "sporting" contest between robots of no interest? Why are women less interested in sport than men?

What the aesthetic approach ignores is the need for heroes that sports satisfy. This need is at its most passionate among boys young enough to have a flourishing fantasy life; I suspect that it is the residue of this juvenile fantasy that fuels adult attachment to sport.

Insofar as I respond to the aesthetic in sport, it is moments of grace (grace: what a complex word!) that I respond to, moments or movements (another interesting word) that cannot be the issue of rational planning but seem to come down as a kind of blessing from on high upon the mortal players, moments when everything goes right, everything clicks into place, when the lookers-on don't even want to applaud, just to give silent thanks that they were there as witnesses.

Yet what athlete would want to be complimented for his grace on the field? Even women athletes would give you a hard look. Grace, gracefulness: effeminate terms.

If I look into my own heart and ask why in the twilight of my days I am still—sometimes—prepared to spend hours watching cricket on television, I must report that, however absurdly, however wistfully, I continue to look out for moments of heroism, moments of nobility. In other words, the basis of my interest is ethical rather than aesthetic.

Absurdly because modern professional sport has no interest in the ethical: it responds to our craving for the heroic only with the spectacle of the heroic. "We cried out for bread and you gave us stones."

The ubiquity of the postgame interview. The man who for an hour or two threatened to leave us behind, to ascend into that realm—only one step short of the divine—where heroes have their being is compelled to resume his mere earthly status, that is to say, is ritually humiliated. "Yeah," he is compelled to say, "we worked hard for this, and it paid off. It was a team effort."

You don't work to become a hero. That is to say, what you do in preparation for the heroic contest is not "work," does not belong to the round of production and consumption. The Spartans at Thermopylae fought together and died together; they were heroes all of them, but they were not a "team" of heroes. A team of heroes is an oxymoron.

All the best,

John

Dear John,

I don't think we are at odds about this. My letter from Paris was mostly a response to your comments about watching sports on television (a narrow topic, no more than a small sub-issue in the very large conversation about sports in general) and why we, supposedly grown men, would choose to fritter away an entire Sunday afternoon following the essentially meaningless activities of young athletes on distant ball fields. A so-called guilty pleasure, but one that often leaves us feeling hollowed out and disgusted with ourselves after the game is over.

Taking the broadest view possible, it strikes me that the subject of sports can be divided into two major categories: the active and the passive. On the one hand, the experience of participating in sports oneself. On the other hand, the experience of watching others play. Since we seem to have begun with a discussion of the latter, I will do my best to confine myself to that part of the question for now.

The ethical component you refer to is especially vital to the very young. You worship your gods and want to emulate them; every contest is a matter of life and death. At my advanced age, however, these attachments have weakened considerably, and I tend to find myself watching games from a much farther remove, looking for "aesthetic pleasures" rather than seeking to validate my own existence through the actions of others. Not to belabor the point, let's drop the old man's perspective for now. Let's go back to the beginning and try to remember what happened to us in the distant past.

Your use of the word "heroic" is fitting and no doubt crucial for understanding the nature of the obsession, which inevitably begins at the dawn of conscious life. But what does it mean to talk about the heroic in connection to early childhood? With young boys, I think, it largely has to do with an idea of the masculine, of sexual identification, of preparing oneself to become a man . . . and not a woman.

Having raised two children—a boy and a girl—I was deeply fascinated (and often highly amused) to watch their sexual identities emerge at around the age of three. In both cases, it began through excess, through intensely exaggerated simulations of what it means to be a man and what it means to be a woman. With the boy, it was all about Superman, the Incredible Hulk, and incorporating imaginary beings who were endowed with magical, all-crushing strength. With the girl (who at two asked if and when she would begin to grow a penis), it manifested itself in party shoes, miniature high heels, tutus, plastic tiaras, and a preoccupation with ballerinas and fairy princesses. Classic stuff, of course, but because it takes a while for boys and girls to understand that they are boys and girls, their first steps toward sexual identification are necessarily extreme, marked by a fixation on the symbols and outer trappings of their sex. Once the issue is settled (around age five?), the girl who previously insisted on wearing dresses at all times could happily put on a pair of pants without fear of turning into a boy.

As an American child in the early 1950s, I began my simulations of masculine life as a cowboy. Again, it was all about the outer trappings—the boots, the hat, the six-shooters snug in their holsters. Because no self-respecting cowboy could possibly go by the name of Paul, whenever I was decked out in my Wild West costume I insisted that my mother call me *John*— and refused to answer her whenever she forgot. (You were never an American cowboy by any chance, were you, John?)

But then—at what moment I can no longer remember, though surely when I was somewhere between four and five— a new passion took hold of me, a new set of symbols, a new realm in which to assert my masculinity. Football (in its American incarnation). I had never played a game, I barely understood the rules, but somewhere, somehow (through photos in newspapers? through games broadcast on TV?), I got it into my head that football players were the true heroes of modern civilization. Once again, it was all about the outer trappings. I didn't want to play football so much as to dress up as a football player, to own a football uniform, and my ever-indulgent mother granted my wish by buying me one. Helmet, shoulder pads and two-color jersey, the special pants that came down to the knee, along with a leather football—which allowed me to look at myself in the mirror and *pretend* that I was a football player. There are even photographs that document the imaginary exploits of that little boy in his pristine uniform which never once touched an actual football field, which was never once worn outside the domain of the small garden apartment he lived in with his parents.

Eventually, of course, I did begin to play football—and baseball as well. With fanatical devotion, I might add, and the more interested I became in doing these things, the more interested I became in following the performances of the great

ones, the professionals. In Portugal, I told you about the auda-
cious, semi-insane letter I wrote to Otto Graham (the finest
quarterback of the period, the star of the champion Cleveland
Browns) inviting him to my eighth birthday party—and the
gracious response I received from him, explaining why he
could not attend. Ever since I mentioned this story to you, I
have continued to ponder it, searching for more details, trying
to come to a deeper understanding of my motives at the time.
I remember now a distinct fantasy of Otto Graham coming to
my house and the two of us going into the backyard and playing catch with a football. That was the birthday party. There
were no other guests present—no other children, not even my
parents—no one but my soon to be eight-year-old self and the
immortal O.G.

I see now, I *know* now with utmost conviction, that this fantasy represented a wish to create a substitute father. In the
America of my young mind, fathers were supposed to play
catch with their sons, but my father rarely did that with me, was
seldom available in any of the ways I imagined fathers were
supposed to be available to their sons, and so I invited a football
hero *to my house* in the vain hope that he could give me whatever it was my own father had failed to give me. Are all heroes
substitute fathers? Is that why boys seem to have a greater need
for heroes than girls? Is all this youthful fixation on sports no
more than another example of the Oedipal struggle gone un-
derground? I'm not sure. But the maniacal intensity of sports
fans—not all, but vast numbers nevertheless—has to come
from somewhere very deep in the soul. There is more at stake
here than momentary diversion or mere entertainment.

I don't mean to suggest that Freud is the only one with

anything to say on the matter, but there is no doubt that he has something to add to the conversation.

I realize that I often respond to your remarks with stories about myself. Understand: I am not interested in myself. I am giving you case studies, stories about anyone.

> With warmest thoughts,
>
> Paul

Dear Paul,

You write of the young male child's fixation on sporting heroes, and go on to distinguish this from a mature attitude that seeks the aesthetic in the sporting spectacle.

Like you, I think that watching sport on television is mostly a waste of time. But there are moments that are not a waste of time, as would for example crop up now and again in the glory days of Roger Federer. In the light of what you say, I scrutinize such moments, revisiting them in memory—Federer playing a cross-court backhand volley, for instance. Is it truly, or only, the aesthetic, I ask myself, that brings such moments alive for me?

It seems to me that two thoughts go through my mind as I watch: (1) If only I had spent my adolescence practicing my backhand instead of . . . then I too could have played shots like that and made people all over the world gasp with wonder; followed by: (2) Even if I had spent the whole of my adolescence practicing my backhand, I would not be able to play that shot, not in the stress of competition, not at will. And therefore: (3) I have just seen something that is at the same time both human and more than human; I have just seen something like the human ideal made visible.

What I would want to note in this set of responses is the way in which envy first raises its head and is then extinguished. One starts by envying Federer, one moves from there to admiring him, and one ends up neither envying nor admiring him but exalted at the revelation of what a human being—a being like oneself—can do.

Which, I find, is very much like my response to master-works of art on which I have spent a lot of time (reflection, analysis), to the point where I have a good idea of what went into their making: I can see how it was done, but I could never have done it myself, it is beyond me; yet it was done by a man (now and again a woman) like me; what an honor to belong to the species that he (occasionally she) exemplifies!

And at that point I can no longer distinguish the ethical from the aesthetic.

As a footnote to my comments on the present banking crisis, may I quote a comment by George Soros that I came across? "The salient feature of the current financial crisis is that it was not caused by some external shock. . . . The crisis was generated by the system itself." Dimly Soros recognizes that nothing has really happened—the only things that have changed are the numbers.

All good wishes,

John

Dear John,

In light of your quotation from George Soros, these sentences from the galleys of a book I received the other day, written by a professor friend, Mark C. Taylor, to be published by Columbia University Press: "Since the late 1970s a new form of capitalism has emerged—finance capitalism. In previous forms of capitalism (i.e., industrial and consumer capitalism), people made money by buying and selling labor or material objects. In finance capitalism, by contrast, wealth is created by circulating signs, backed by nothing but other signs, in a regression that for practical purposes is limitless. Financial markets have become a sophisticated confidence game, and the people at the helm are latter-day versions of Melville's wily Confidence Man. . . ."

·

A new twist in the Beckett Chronicle that might amuse you. A couple of weeks ago I received an invitation to attend a new literary festival to be held just outside Dublin in September and to give—imagine this—the first annual Samuel Beckett Address. I tortured myself about it for several days and then finally agreed to accept the invitation. I hope I haven't made a terrible mistake. I wish, somehow, that we could do it in tandem.

On the subject, I bought a copy of the first volume of Beckett's letters last week and have been poking around in it with a kind of gloomy fascination. Never have I seen a book of correspondence with such a heavy, cumbersome apparatus. I now understand your doubts and confusions when you were asked to review it. The distinction between "work" and "life" has created a volume in which too much is missing, and I feel frustrated by it and at times (I confess) rather bored. I'm looking forward to reading your piece.

·

We can leave sports behind if you wish, although I was planning to go on at great length about the second part of the question (participating in sports rather than watching others play them): the pleasures of competition, the intense focus required that at times enables you to transcend the strictures of your own consciousness, the concept of belonging to a team, the necessity of coping with failure, and numerous other topics. At some later point, perhaps, I will sit down and try to write that letter, even if we are in the midst of something else. It's a subject that still interests me a great deal.

As for the exaltation you talk about when watching Federer in his glory days, I am in total accord with you. Awe at the fact that a fellow human being is accomplishing such things, that we (as a species) are not only the worms we often appear to be but are also capable of achieving miraculous things—in tennis, in music, in poetry, in science—and that envy and admiration dissolve into a feeling of overwhelming joy. Yes, I agree with you entirely. And that is where the aesthetic and the ethical merge. I have no counter-argument, for I have often felt exactly the same way myself.

> With fondest good thoughts,
>
> Paul

Dear Paul,

Before you tell me what you think of the pleasures of competition, I have a preemptive comment to make.

In my early twenties I was deeply involved in chess. For years I had been spending my working days writing machine code for computers, getting so deeply sucked into the process that I sometimes felt I was descending into a madness in which the brain is taken over by mechanical logic.

I had the good sense to abandon computers, and then made my way to the United States to do a graduate degree. Onboard ship crossing the Atlantic (yes, in those days one could travel by sea if one didn't have much money—the crossing took five days) I entered a chess competition and made it through to the final round, where my opponent was to be an engineering student from Germany named Robert.

Our match commenced at midnight. At dawn we were still hunched over the chessboard. Robert was one piece up, but I felt I had the tactical advantage. The last few spectators around the board drifted away: they wanted to get a sight of the Statue of Liberty. Robert and I were alone.

"I'll give you a draw," Robert offered. "OK," I said. We stood up, shook hands, put away the chess set.

He was a piece up, but I had the advantage: a draw was a fair compromise, not so?

We docked. I was in the legendary city of New York. But the mood of the contest would not leave me, a mood of cerebral excitement, feverish and slightly sick, like a real inflammation of the brain. I had no interest in my surroundings. Something kept humming inside me.

My wife and I got through Customs and found our way to the bus station. We were to catch different buses: she would go to Georgia to stay with friends while I went to Austin to find a place for us to live. I said good-bye to her abstractedly. All I wanted was to be alone, so that I could replay the chess game on paper and settle the doubt that nagged me. All the way to Texas in the Greyhound bus (two days? three days?) I pored over my notations, following a hunch that I should never have accepted a draw, that in three or four or five moves Robert the German would have been forced to capitulate.

I should have been drinking in my first sights of the New World. I should have been making plans for the new life that was opening up before me. But no, I was in the grip of a fever. In a quiet way, I was raving mad. I was the madman in the last row of the bus.

That episode is what comes to mind when you write about the pleasures of competition. What I associate with competition is not pleasure at all but a state of possession in which the mind is focused on a single absurd goal: to defeat some stranger in whom one has no interest, whom one has never seen before and will never see again.

The memory of undergoing that fit of nasty exultation, nearly half a century ago, has fortified me forever against wanting to be the winner at all costs, to defeat some or other opponent and come out on top. I have never played chess since then. I have played sports (tennis, cricket), I have done a lot of cycling, but in all of this my aspiration has simply been to do as well as I can. Winning or losing—who cares? How I judge whether or not I have done well is a private matter, between myself and what I suppose I would call my conscience.

I don't like forms of sport that model themselves too closely on warfare, in which all that matters is winning and winning becomes a matter of life and death—sports that lack grace, as war lacks grace. At the back of my mind is some ideal—and perhaps concocted—vision of Japan in which one refrains from inflicting defeat on an opponent because there is something shameful in defeat and therefore something shameful in imposing defeat.

All the best,

John

Paul Auster and J. M. Coetzee

Dear John,

I have been living in a state of gloom and sorrow these past months. It has been a season of death, a time of funerals, memorial services, and condolence letters, and even as the headlines announce the disintegration of our flawed and ragged world, these private losses have touched me far more deeply than the mayhem burning in the universe-at-large.

On Christmas day, the suicide of the twenty-three-year-old daughter of one of my oldest friends. In February, the death of a beloved woman friend I had known since I was seventeen. And last month, the absurd death of a forty-five-year-old friend after what appeared to be a harmless fall. All women, all gone before they could live out the time allotted to most of us. I tell myself that I should know better than to feel surprised, that such is the way of the world, that we are all mortal beings and our end can come at any time, but the long view offers not the smallest shred of consolation. The heart aches. There is simply no cure for it.

Your chess story—which is also a kind of horror story—has made me rethink what I mean by the word "competition."

(I haven't played chess in years, by the way, but there was a time in my early twenties when I became immersed in it, too. It is without question the most obsessive, most mentally damaging game invented by man. After a while, I found myself dreaming about chess moves in my sleep—and decided that I had to stop playing or else go mad.)

When I used the phrase "the pleasures of competition," I

think I was referring to the sense of release that comes from giving yourself wholly to a game, the beneficial effect on both body and mind caused by absolute concentration on a particular task at a particular moment, the sense of being "outside yourself," temporarily relieved of the burden of self-consciousness. Winning and losing are necessary but secondary factors, the excuse one needs in order to make a maximum effort to play well—for without maximum effort, there can be no real pleasure.

Exercise for the sake of exercise has always bored me. Sit-ups and push-ups, jogging around the track "to stay in shape," lifting weights, tossing around a medicine ball do not have the same salutary effect produced by competition. By trying to win the game you are playing, you forget that you are running and jumping, forget that you are actually getting a healthy dose of exercise. You have lost yourself in what you are doing, and for reasons I don't fully understand, this seems to bring intense happiness. There are other transcendent human activities, of course—sex being one of them, making art another, experiencing art yet another, but the fact is that the mind sometimes wanders during sex—which is not always transcendent!—making art (think: writing novels) is filled with doubts, pauses, and erasures, and we are not always able to give our full attention to the Shakespeare sonnet we are reading or the Bach oratorio we are listening to. If you are not fully in the game you are playing, however, you are not truly playing it.

We mustn't overlook the question of fatigue. If your body tires in the middle of a game, you lose your concentration and your desire to win (that is, the ability to make a maximum effort). That is why tough and demanding competitive sports are played by young people, why most professional athletes are finished by the time they reach their midthirties. But there is a definite pleasure in trying to push yourself beyond your perceived limits, of continuing to make a maximum effort even though your resources are spent.

I vividly remember my last stab at sporting glory. Twenty-plus years ago, I played in the New York Publishers Softball League once a week in Central Park as a member of the Viking-Penguin team (your American publisher, formerly mine). The squads were coed, the games were loose, sloppy affairs, but even though I was pushing forty or already past it, I enjoyed reactivating my old baseball muscles and (by force of habit and temperament) always played hard. One evening, as I stood at my position in the field (third base), the batter lofted a foul ball far, far to my right. When I saw the trajectory of the ball, I understood that I had no chance of catching it, but (again, by force of habit and temperament) I went after it anyway. Urging my no longer young legs to move as quickly as they could, I ran for what felt like ten minutes, realized that yes, perhaps I did have a chance, and at the last moment, just as the ball was about to hit the ground, lunged at full extension, snagged the ball in the utmost tip of my glove, and belly-flopped onto the grass. Remember, this was a game of no account, a friendly contest between joking book editors, secretaries, receptionists, and mailroom clerks, and yet I willed myself to go after that ball from a simple desire to push myself, to see if I had it in me to catch it. I was out of breath, of course, my knees and elbows were smarting, but I felt happy, terribly and stupidly happy.

Which is to say, I am with you. The idea is not to win but to do well, to do the best you can. Your chess match with the stranger on the ship brought you face-to-face with some demonic part of yourself, and when you saw what you had become, you recoiled in disgust. I have never had a similar revelation. I don't think, in fact, that I have ever been as hungry to win a match of any kind as you were with that German fellow in 1965. Does it have something to do with the difference between team sports and individual sports? All through my boyhood and adolescence I played on teams (primarily baseball and basketball) but rarely competed in one-on-one activities (running, boxing, tennis). Of all the hundreds of games I participated in, I would guess my teams won and lost in roughly equal measure. Winning was always more enjoyable than losing, of course, but I can't remember ever feeling devastated by a loss—except for the few times when I bungled a crucial play and felt responsible for letting down my teammates.

In individual sports, however, I imagine the ego must be far more significantly engaged—and far more at risk. Hence your compulsive replaying of the chess match on that gruesome bus ride to Texas. You felt you were the better player, then *proved* you were, and cursed yourself for having accepted a draw. But what happens when the opposite is true, when you know you are *not* the better player?

I am thinking of tennis, a sport I never spent much time with and am not very good at (awful backhand)—but which I nevertheless like to play. My father, who lived and breathed tennis, whose very existence was defined by his love of tennis (for many years, he would wake at six in the morning in order to play for a couple of hours before going to work), could still beat me most of the time when he was in his sixties and I was

Paul Auster and J. M. Coetzee

in my twenties. Even though I knew I probably couldn't win, I always gave maximum effort when we played and measured my successes by how long I could keep volleys going, by how much I felt my game was improving, etc. Losses never stung. On the other hand, I have found that some victories are empty, even distasteful. About fifteen or eighteen years ago, I once played tennis with a writer friend, who turned out to be so bad at it, so tragically inept, that he didn't manage to win a single point against me. I felt no pleasure in winning. I merely felt sorry for my poor, brave opponent, who had jumped into the deep end of the pool without knowing how to swim.

The pleasure of competition, therefore, is most keen when the opponents are evenly matched.

With best thoughts,

Paul

Dear Paul,

Thank you for sending me *Invisible*, which I read in two long sessions—two gulps, as it were.

You told me last November that there would be incest in your next book, but I didn't appreciate—given the added complication you introduce, namely the question *Where does the act of incest take place, in the bed or in the mind or in the writing?*—how close to the heart of the book incest would be.

It's an interesting subject, incest, one to which I have not given much conscious thought until now (how would one dare to deny, post Freud, that one has not given it unconscious thought?). It strikes me as curious that, even in the popular tongue, we use the same denomination for sex between brother and sister as for sex between father and daughter or mother and son (let's put aside the various homosexual combinations for the moment). It's hard to experience the same frisson of repugnance about the first as about the latter two. I don't have a sister, but I find it all too easy to imagine how alluring sex games might be to a brother and a sister of more or less the same age—sex games proceeding to more than sex games, as in your book. Whereas sex with one's own offspring must seem quite a step to take. I would have thought we would have developed different terms for two very different moral acts.

There was a case last year in rural South Australia in which a father-daughter couple who had been living for decades as man and wife in fairly isolated circumstances were prosecuted.

I don't remember all the details, but the court ordered that they be separated, the father/husband being enjoined not to come anywhere near his daughter/wife under threat of a jail term. It seemed to me a cruel punishment, given that the complaint had come not from either of the partners but from neighbors.

Having sex with one's parents or children must be just about the last sexual taboo that survives in our society. (I confidently predict that *Invisible* will not be greeted with howls of outrage, confirming my sense that brother-sister sex is OK, at least to talk about and write about.) We have come a long way from societies divided into castes within which sexual relations had to be confined. I suppose that the arrival of easy contraception marked the demise of sexual taboos: the bugaboo that the woman might give birth to a monster lost its force.

Not enough attention has been given, I think, to the role that the lore of animal husbandry played in the creation of sexual and racial taboos—lore dictating what species might be allowed to mate with what other species, or within a bloodline how many degrees of separation there had to be, evolved in the course of hundreds of generations of stock raising.

Anyway, today pretty much everything seems to go. The righteous fury that used to be able to play over a whole range of tabooed sex acts (including adultery!) has been focused on a single act, namely grown men having sex with children, which is, I suppose, our way of extending the coverage of the father-child taboo.

Interesting that when in benighted corners of the world (most notably benighted corners of the Muslim world) adulterous couples are punished, we criticize the law that punishes them for ignoring their human rights. What kind of world are we living in in which it is our *right* to break a taboo? What is the point of having a taboo (your Byronic Adam Walker might ask) if it is OK to violate it?

All the best,

John

Paul Auster and J. M. Coetzee

Dear John,

So happy that *Invisible* reached you and that you have consumed it so quickly.

No, I haven't given much conscious thought to the subject of incest either—at least not until I wrote the novel. Unlike you, I do have a sister, but she is nearly four years younger than I am, and the thought of going down that road with her never once crossed my mind. On the other hand, when I was eighteen or nineteen, I dreamed one night that I was making love to my mother. The dream baffled me then and continues to baffle me today, since it seems to demolish the classic Freudian equation: sublimation of desires through cryptic symbols and often oblique imagery, each thing standing in for something else. His theory has no place for what I experienced. As I recall, I was not disturbed by what was happening inside the dream, but after I woke up I was shocked and revolted.

Shocked because at bottom I suppose I accept the taboo as inviolate. Not just incest between parents and children but between brother and sister as well. Whether what happens in my book with Walker and Gwyn really happens is open to question, but I had to write those passages from a position of absolute belief, and I confess that it was difficult for me—as if I had cut through the barbed-wire fence that stands between sanity and the darkness of transgression. And yet I fully agree with you that the book will not be met with howls of outrage (at least not on that count!). In fact, I think I already have proof of that. Earlier this week, Siri and I did a joint reading at Brown

University in Providence at the invitation of Robert Coover (an old friend whom we hadn't seen in a while). I read some pages from the second part (which included the "grand experiment" but not the full-bore incest of 1967), and although Siri reported that some students tittered nervously behind her, after the reading was over not a single person mentioned those paragraphs. "Nice reading," they said, or "Very interesting, can't wait to read the book," but nothing about the content of what they had heard.

Bouncing off your remarks about animal husbandry, I was reminded of a book I translated many years ago by the French anthropologist Pierre Clastres—*Chronicle of the Guayaki Indians*—an excellent, beautifully written study of a small, primitive tribe living in the jungles of South America. There is one homosexual in the group, Krembegi, and this is the astonishing account of what person(s) he can sleep with—and why:

> The ultimate bases of Atchei (Guayaki) social life are the alliances between family groups, relations that take form and are fulfilled in marriage exchanges, in the continual exchange of women. A woman exists in order to circulate, to become the wife of a man who is not her father, her brother, or her son. It is in this manner that one makes Picha, allies. But can a man, even one who exists as a woman, "circulate?" How could the gift of Krembegi, for example, be paid back? This was not even imaginable, since he was not a woman, but a homosexual. The chief law of all societies is the prohibition against incest. Because he was kyrypy-meno—

(literally, an anus-lovemaker)—Krembegi was outside this social order. In his case, the logic of the social system—or, what amounts to the same thing, the logic of its reversal—was worked out to its very end: Krembegi's partners were his own brothers. 'Picha kybai (meaning kyrypy-meno) menoia.' "A kyrypy-meno man does not make love with his allies." This injunction is the exact opposite of the rules governing the relations between men and women. Homosexuality can only be "incestuous"; the brother sodomizes his brother, and in this metaphor of incest the certainty that there can never be any real incest (between a man and a woman) without destroying the social body is confirmed and reinforced.

Extraordinary, no? Encouraging incest in order to discourage it. The head spins . . .

On another note, I want to congratulate you on your piece for the *New York Review* on Beckett's letters. Thorough, compassionate, and just. Siri was especially pleased by the space you devoted to Bion. In the wake of your article and in anticipation of the talk I have agreed to deliver in Ireland this coming September, I dutifully plowed through the book, and now that I have come to the end, I want to revise my earlier comments to you. It is not boring. Far from it, and what moved me most was to watch his slow and painful evolution from an arrogant, know-it-all prick into a grounded human being. A note to one of the last letters (the book is not in front of me, so my wording might be off) quotes a letter from Maria Jolas to her husband in which she says something like: Beckett is better now—implying, I think, that they never cared for him personally and were now beginning to change their opinion.

And yes, the notes represent an extraordinary undertaking. But do we really have to be told that Harpo Marx's real name was Arthur?

Best thoughts,

Paul

Paul Auster and J. M. Coetzee

Dear Paul,

One further remark on sport: most of the major sports—
those that draw masses of spectators and arouse mass passions—seem to have been selected and codified in a spurt
around the end of the nineteenth century, in England. What
strikes me is how difficult it is to invent and launch a thoroughly new sport (not just a variant of an old one), or perhaps I
should say launch a new game (sports being selected out of the
repertoire of games). Human beings are ingenious creatures,
yet it is as though only a few of the many possible games (physical games, not games in the head) turn out to be viable.

I have been reading Jacques Derrida's little book on the
mother tongue (*Monolingualism of the Other,* 1996). Some of it
is high theorizing, some quite autobiographical, about Derrida's relations with language as a child born into the Jewish-
French or Jewish French or French-speaking Jewish community
in Algeria in the 1930s. (He reminds us that French citizens of
Jewish inheritance were stripped of their citizenship by Vichy,
and were therefore in fact stateless for several years.)

What interests me is Derrida's claim that, though he is/was
monolingual in French (monolingual by his own standards—
his English was excellent, as, I am sure, was his German, to
say nothing of his Greek), French is/was not his mother tongue.
When I read this it struck me that he could have been writing
about me and my relation to English; and a day later it struck
me further that neither he nor I is exceptional, that many writers and intellectuals have a removed or interrogative relation
to the language they speak and write, in fact that referring to

the language one uses as one's mother tongue (*langue mater-nelle*) has become distinctly old-fashioned.

So when Derrida writes that, though he loves the French language and is a stickler for correct French, it does not belong to him, is not "his," I am reminded of my own experience of English, particularly in childhood. English was to me simply one of my list of school subjects. In senior school the list was English-Afrikaans-Latin-Mathematics-History-Geography, and English happened to be a subject I was good at, Geography a subject I was bad at. It never occurred to me to think that I was good at English because English was "my" language; it certainly never occurred to me to inquire how one could be bad at English if English was one's mother tongue (decades later, after I had become, of all things, a professor of English, and begun to reflect a little on the history of my discipline, I did ask myself what it could possibly mean to make English into an academic subject in an English-speaking country).

Insofar as I can recover my childhood way of thinking, I thought of the English language as the property of the English, people who lived in England but who had also sent out members of their tribe to live in and, for a while, rule over South Africa. The English made up the rules of English as they whimsically chose, including the pragmatic rules (in what situations you had to use what English locutions); people like myself followed at a distance and behaved as instructed. Being good at English was as inexplicable as being bad at geography. It was some quirk of character, of mental makeup.

When at the age of twenty-one I went to live in England, it was with an attitude toward the language that now seems to me exceedingly odd. On the one hand I was pretty sure that by textbook standards I could speak, or at least write, the language better than most of the natives. On the other hand, as soon as I opened my mouth I betrayed myself as a foreigner, that is to say, someone who by definition could not know the language as well as the natives.

I resolved this paradox by distinguishing between two kinds of knowledge. I told myself that I knew English in the same way that Erasmus knew Latin, out of books; whereas the people all around me knew the language "in their bones." It was their mother tongue as it was not mine; they had imbibed it with their mothers' milk, I had not.

Of course to a linguist, and particularly to a linguist in the Chomskyan line, my attitude was completely wrongheaded. The language that you internalize during your receptive early years is your mother tongue, and that is that.

As Derrida remarks, how can one ever conceive of a language as one's own? English may not after all be the property of the English of England, but it is certainly not my property. Language is always the language of the other. Wandering into language is always a trespass. And how much worse if you are good enough at English to hear in every phrase that falls from your pen echoes of earlier usages, reminders of who owned the phrase before you!

All the best,

John

May 11, 2009

Dear John,

Thank you for yesterday's fax. I feel that we have finally hit upon a workable system. A slow letter across the seas from America to Australia and then a quick, electronic transmission of paper from a room in a house in Adelaide to a room in a house in Brooklyn.

The conversation about sports might well be coming to an end, but the question about why no new games have taken hold for so many years is a good one, something, I frankly confess, it has never occurred to me to ask. You mention England and the end of the nineteenth century, but the same applies to America as well. The first professional baseball team was created in 1869, which was the same year that Princeton and Rutgers played the first intercollegiate football match. The only exception I can think of is basketball, which wasn't invented until 1891 and didn't become popular until forty years later when a rules change eliminated the center jump after each basket and speeded up the tempo of the game. Now basketball is played in every country of the world, and just as England no longer owns cricket and soccer, America no longer owns basketball. Case in point: two or three years ago, an overpaid, overconfident American national team lost to Greece in the semifinal of the world championship.

But essentially you are right. Nothing new has made an impact for generations. When you think about how quickly various technologies have altered daily life (trains, cars, airplanes, movies, radios, televisions, computers), the intractability of sports is at first glance mystifying. There has to be a reason for it, though, and the answer that leaps to mind is that, once codified, sports cease to be inventions and turn into institutions. Institutions exist to perpetuate themselves, and the only way they can be eliminated is through revolution. So much is at stake now in professional sports, so much money is involved, there is so much profit to be gained by fielding a successful team that the men who control soccer, basketball, and all other major sports are as powerful as the heads of the largest corporations, the heads of governments. There is simply no room to introduce a new game. The market is saturated, and the games that already exist have become monopolies that will do everything possible to crush any upstart competitor. That doesn't mean that people don't invent new games (children do it every day), but children don't have the wherewithal to launch multi-million-dollar commercial enterprises.

About twenty years ago, I was watching the evening news, and a story came on about a small town somewhere in the south whose board of education—because of budget difficulties, I think—had decided to dispense with the teaching of foreign languages. A number of local citizens were interviewed on camera and asked to give their reactions to this new development, and one man said—and this is an exact quote; his words burned themselves into my brain and have been lodged there ever since—: "I have no problem with it, no problem at all. If English was good enough for Jesus, it's good enough for me."

Stupid and disturbing as that comment might be (and hilarious, too, of course), it seems to touch on something essential about the idea of a mother tongue. You are so thoroughly impregnated by your own language, your sense of the world is so deeply formed by the language you speak, that anyone who does not speak as you do is considered a barbarian—or, conversely, it is inconceivable to you that the son of God could have spoken a language other than your own, for he is the world, and the world exists in one language only, the one that happens to be yours.

Just three generations ago, my great-grandparents spoke Russian, Polish, and Yiddish. That I was raised in an English-speaking country strikes me as a wholly contingent fact, a fluke of history. My father's mother—my demented, homicidal grandmother—spent most of her life in America but spoke English with such a thick accent that I had trouble understanding her. The only thing I ever saw her read was the *Daily Forward*, a newspaper printed in Yiddish. Even more interesting is the case of Siri's father. A third-generation Norwegian-American born in 1922, he grew up in such an isolated rural community—largely inhabited by Norwegian immigrants and their descendants—that all his life he spoke English with a distinctive Norwegian brogue. What was his mother tongue? Siri's Norwegian-born mother didn't move to this country until she was thirty, and because *her* mother came to stay with the Hustvedts in Minnesota after Siri was born (which meant that Norwegian temporarily became the language of the household), the first language Siri spoke was Norwegian. What is her mother tongue? She is an American, a superb writer whose medium is the English language, and yet every now and then she will make a small slip, mostly to do with prepositions (the most daunting element of any language). Water under the bridge. Water over the dam. The two expressions mean the same thing: it's all in the past. But Siri is the only person who has ever said: Water over the bridge.

You were born in a bilingual country, which complicates matters considerably. But if you spoke English at home when you were a child, then you are first and foremost an English speaker. South African English, later tempered by your long stays in the lands of British English, American English, and Australian English. There is also Irish English, Indian English, Caribbean English, and God knows what else. Just as the English no longer own cricket and soccer, they no longer own English. Laugh at the notion of "American" if you will, but the fact is that when the French publish books by American writers, the title page reads: *traduit de l'americain*, not *traduit de l'anglais*. I have many grievances against America, but English in its American incarnation is not one of them.

On the other hand, we who are writers—no matter what our language—should take heart from these words by Groucho Marx: "Outside of a dog, a book is a man's best friend. Inside of a dog, it's too dark to read." I am referring, of course, to Harpo's brother. Whose real name was Julius.

With warmest greetings to you and Dorothy,

Paul

Dear Paul,

You say that the title pages of French translations of your books read, *Traduit de l'americain*. Mine say *Traduit de l'anglais (Sud-Africaine)*. I'd like someone to point to the moments when my *anglais* becomes *sud-africaine*. To me it reads like *anglais* purged of markers of national origin, and a little bloodless for that reason.

I think I am at odds with you over the question of mother tongue (though I note that you tend to eschew that rather feeling-laden phrase in favor of "first language"). I agree that one's weltanschauung is formed by the language that one speaks and writes most easily and, to a degree, thinks in. But it is not formed so deeply that one can never stand far enough outside that language to inspect it critically—particularly if one speaks or even just understands another language. That is why I say that it is possible to have a first language yet nonetheless not feel at home in it: it is, so to speak, one's primary tongue but not one's mother tongue.

This phenomenon is more widespread than one might think. In Europe, for instance, before the arrival of the nation-state and the triumph of national languages, Latin—which was no one's mother tongue—was the currency of intellectual life. The same situation exists in Africa today vis-à-vis English and (to a lesser extent) French and Portuguese. In Africa it is not practically possible to be an intellectual in your mother tongue; you can't even be much of a writer. In India and Pakistan, where it is the home language of only a minuscule minority, English is the medium of much of literature and all of science.

You point out that there is such a thing as American English or Indian English, and imply that these "Englishes" have mother-tongue status in the United States and India respectively. But the truth is that *on the page* (leave aside *in the mouth* or *in the street*) these differ from English only in trivial respects: the odd locution or idiom here and there, not the elemental vocabulary (which has such determinative power over the speaker's epistemology) or the syntax (which dictates the forms of thought).

As I said, I started thinking about the subject of the mother tongue after reading Derrida. I began to feel my own situation more acutely after moving to Australia, which—despite the fact that within its territory there are scores of Aboriginal languages still clinging to life, and despite the fact that since 1945 it has encouraged massive immigration from southern Europe and Asia—is far more "English" than my native South Africa. In Australia public life is monolingual. More important, relations to reality are mediated in a notably uninterrogated way through a single language, English.

The effect on me of living in an environment so saturated with English has been a peculiar one: it has created more and more of a skeptical distance between myself and what I would loosely call the Anglo weltanschauung, with its inbuilt templates of how one thinks, how one feels, how one relates to other people, and so forth.

All the best,

John

Dear Paul,

Last month I visited your country for the first time in five years, to see my brother, who lives in Washington, D.C., and has been ill.

Before embarking I very deliberately thought through the question of first impressions and what I was going to allow to count as first impressions; in particular, whether I was going to allow your immigration service, recently rebranded as Homeland Security, to play any role in forming them.

For, as you know, I have a long and largely unhappy history of relations with U.S. Immigration, which I won't rehearse. I was not eager to be plunged back into that history and have my mood touched by its sourness.

In the event, the immigration interview at Los Angeles airport was as bad as I had feared. I was escorted out of the line and taken to a back office, where for an hour I waited my turn among the mail-order brides and students with papers from dubious colleges, before being quizzed by a poker-faced officer: Who was I? Had I visited the U.S. before, and if so when? The interrogation went on and on, in circles. "If you will just tell me what the problem is," I said at one point, "then I can perhaps try to solve it for you." "Sorry, sir," replied the officer, "I am not at liberty to divulge that."

In the end they stamped my passport and let me in. What it was all about I still don't know. Perhaps I was just an elderly

* A letter that went astray and didn't reach Auster, which accounts for his failure to answer it.

Caucasian randomly pulled out of the arrivals line to prove it is not only young men "of Middle Eastern appearance" who get harassed.

"I am not at liberty to tell you what is wrong." It can't be much fun having to parrot such gobbledygook. But who would want to work for a service where you earn promotion not for the number of people you let through but for the number you turn back?

But I was going to write about first impressions, not about immigration officials and their discontents. I was going to give you my first impressions of America after a long absence. Yet what strikes me now is how banal those first impressions were, and more generally how little of interest I have to say about foreign places, despite a lifetime of traveling.

France, for instance: even after having wound my way around most of France on a bicycle, I can't claim to have anything to say about the country that is fresh, new, worth saying. England, where I lived for years, or America, where I lived even longer, ditto. To say nothing about South Africa, where I was formed and spent most of my working life, or Australia, where I have lived for the past seven years. Memories, plenty of memories. Images, some of them quite vivid. But all of them trapped in their particularity, not generalizable. My experiences seem to remain my experiences alone, not relevant to other people.

I seem to be afflicted with a peculiar kind of blindness. It's not that I am incurious. On the contrary, everywhere I go my eyes are wide open, I am on the alert for signs. But the signs I pick up seem to have no general meaning. And the generalizability of the particular is the essence of realism, is it not? I have in mind realism as a way of seeing the world and recording it in such a way that particulars, though captured in all their uniqueness, seem yet to have meaning, to belong to a coherent system.

What does a phenomenon like this mean: a more or less intelligent person like myself living in an age of easy travel, who as he nears the end of his life must recognize that his manifold experience of the visible world adds up to nothing worth retelling, that he might as well have spent his life in a library?

Or is it perhaps that I have been picking up the wrong sort of signs—that the only signs I see, because of my idiosyncratic blindness, are signs that tell me that life is the same everywhere in the world, rather than signs of the distinctiveness of every tiny part of creation?

If the born travel writer is preternaturally alert to signs of difference, am I the born anti–travel writer, alert only to signs of the same?

The whole business puzzles me. I say to myself, *You have just come back from a visit to the United States, what were your impressions?* And again and again, blocking out every other image, comes a memory of a young man in nondescript clothing riding a battered old bicycle, nonchalantly, in the wrong direction, against the traffic, in a Manhattan street. What does it mean, this solitary, overriding image? Why, when I say to myself *Give your impressions* or *Summon up your images*, is this the only image that comes back? Is there some absurd faculty inside me trying to tell me the young man riding the wrong way says something about America in 2009?

I travel but don't write travel books. Nor do you; or perhaps you do, but publish them under a pseudonym: Peter Westermann, Nicole Brebis. Do you have first impressions that you trust? I don't trust mine in the slightest.

Yours ever,

John

Dear Paul,

I have been thinking about names, about their fittingness or unfittingness. I would guess that names interest you too, if only because of having to find good, "right" names for your imaginary persons. Neither of us seems to go in for calling characters A or B or Pim or Bom.

I was brought up within the linguistic orthodoxy that the signifier is arbitrary, though for mysterious reasons the signifiers of one language won't work as signifiers in another language (*Help me, I am dying of thirst!* will get you nowhere in Mongolia). This is supposed to be doubly true of proper names: whether a street is named Marigold Street or Mandragora Street or indeed Fifty-fifth Street is supposed to make no difference (no practical difference).

In the realm of poetry (in the widest sense) the doctrine of the arbitrariness of the signifier has never won much credence. In poetry the connotations of words—the accumulations of cultural significance around them—matter. "Mandragora," via Keats, calls up bliss and death. "Fifty-fifth Street," which at first sight seems anonymous, turns out to connote anonymity.

Through a supreme act of poetic power, Franz Kafka has given a letter of the alphabet allusive (connotative) force. Roberto Calasso's recent book is called simply *K*. We look at the jacket and we know what it will be about.

I once called a character K (Michael K) as a stroke to reclaim the letter of the alphabet that Kafka had annexed, but didn't have much success.

Few of us write novels, but most of us, one way or another,

end up producing offspring, and are then compelled by law to give our offspring names. There are parents who accept this duty with joy, and parents who accept it with misgiving. There are parents who feel free to make up a name as they choose, and parents constrained (by law, by custom, by anxiety) to choose a name from a list.

Parents with misgivings try to give the child a neutral name, a name without connotations, a name that will not embarrass it in later life. Thus: Enid.

But there is a catch. Name too many daughters Enid, and the name Enid comes to signify the kind of child whose parents reacted with misgiving to the duty of naming a child and thus gave their girl-child as anonymous a name as they could. So "Enid" becomes a kind of fatality awaiting the child as she grows up: diffidence, caution, reserve.

Or someone far away, someone you have never heard of, disgraces your name. You grow up in the Midwest of the United States, and everything is fine until one day someone asks you, "Are you by any chance related to Adolf Hitler?" and you have to change your name by deed poll to Hilter or Hiller or Smith.

Your name is your destiny. Oidipous, Swollen-foot. The only trouble is, your name speaks your destiny only in the way the Delphic Sibyl does: in the form of a riddle. Only as you lie on your deathbed do you realize what it meant to be "Tamerlane" or "John Smith" or "K." A Borgesian revelation.

All the best,

John

Dear John,

First, allow me to pounce on Fifty-fifth Street—which "turns out to connote anonymity." For the sake of argument, let us assume that the Fifty-fifth Street in question happens to be located in New York, the borough of Manhattan to be precise, east side or west side not indicated, but Midtown Manhattan for all that, and then anyone who lives in this city will be able to conjure up vivid mental pictures and a flood of personal memories about that street whose name is not a word but an anonymous number. You write "Fifty-fifth Street," and I immediately think about the St. Regis Hotel and an erotic encounter I had there when I was young, about taking the French writer Edmond Jabès and his wife there for tea one afternoon and seeing Arthur Ashe enter the room in his tennis whites, about lunching there with Vanessa Redgrave and discussing the role she was about to play in my film, *Lulu on the Bridge*. The numbers tell stories, and behind the blank wall of their anonymity they are just as alive and evocative as the Elysian Fields of Paris. Mention to a New Yorker the following streets, and his mind will swarm with images: 4th Street (Greenwich Village), 14th Street (the cheapest stores in the city), 34th Street (Herald Square, Macy's, illuminated Christmas decorations), 42nd Street (Times Square, "legitimate" theaters, Give my regards to Broadway), 59th Street (the Plaza Hotel and the grand entrance to Central Park), 125th Street (Harlem, the Apollo Theater, Duke Ellington's song about the A train). Just two blocks up from 55th Street, on West 57th, there is the building in which my grandfather used to have his office (intense childhood memories of going in there and being allowed to play with the typewriters and adding machines), which happens to be the same building that for many years housed the *New York Review of Books* (intense memories from early adulthood of sitting with Bob Silvers as we discussed the pieces I had written for him)—so that the mere mention of 57th Street will summon forth for me an entire archeology of my past, memories layered on top of other memories, the primordial dig.

And yet, as you say, the signifier is arbitrary, and until or unless that signifier is filled up with personal associations, it will remain indistinguishable from any other signifier. Just the other day, when Siri and I returned from Nantucket (that is, before I had read your letter), the taxi driver from the airport took a shortcut through a Brooklyn neighborhood I was not familiar with, and as we rode down Ocean Parkway, we traversed twenty-six consecutive cross streets named after the letters of the alphabet, from Avenue A to Avenue Z, and I remember thinking that none of this meant anything to me, that unlike the Avenue A in Manhattan (the East Village), which I know and therefore have a personal connection to, the Avenue A in Brooklyn is a complete cipher. I found myself pondering how boring it would be to live on a street named Avenue E or Avenue L. On the other hand, I also thought: Avenue K wouldn't be bad (for all the reasons you mention), and other interesting or tolerable letters would be O, X, and Z—the nothing, the unknown, and the end. Then I walked into the house, which is also on a street designated by a number, and read your fax about K and 55th Street. Perfect timing.

The first book published by George Oppen, the American

poet I am so fond of, was called *Discrete Series* (circa 1930)—a mathematical term, as I'm sure you know, and the example Oppen always gave to describe a discrete series was this: 4, 14, 23, 34, 42, 59, 66, 72. . . . At first glance, a meaningless collection of numbers, but when you learn that those numbers are in fact the station stops along the IRT subway line in Manhattan, they take on the force of lived experience. Arbitrary, yes, but at the same time not meaningless.

Many years ago, when I wrote my little novel *Ghosts*, I gave all the characters the names of colors: Black, White, Green, Blue, Brown, etc. Yes, I wanted to give the story an abstract, fable-like quality, but at the same time I was also thinking about the irreducibility of colors, that the only way we can know and understand what colors are is to experience them, that to describe "blue" or "green" to a blind man is something beyond the power of language, and that just as colors are irreducible and indescribable, so too are people, and we can never know or understand anything about a person until we "experience" that person, in the same way we can be said to experience colors.

We grow into the names we are given, we test them out, we grapple with them until we come to accept that we are the names we bear. Can you remember practicing your signature as a young boy? Not long after we learn how to write in longhand, most children spend hours filling up pieces of paper with their names. It is not an empty pursuit. It is an attempt, I feel, to convince ourselves that we and our names are one, to take on an identity in the eyes of the world.

In some cultures, people are given new names after reaching puberty, at times even a third name after committing a great or ignominious deed in adulthood.

Some people, of course, are saddled with atrocious names, comical names, deeply unfortunate names. The most pathetic one I have ever run across belonged to a man who married a distant relative: Elmer Deutlebaum. Imagine walking through life as Elmer Deutlebaum.

My Canadian-born grandfather, the son of Polish-Jewish immigrants, out of some incomprehensible loyalty to the British crown, named my mother Queenie. It took her many years to grow into that one. When she was eight or nine, after years of teasing from her classmates, she decided to change it to Estelle. Not as bland as Enid, perhaps, but hardly an improvement. The experiment lasted for approximately six months.

Not to be forgotten in all this is our common ancestor, Adam. According to the Old Testament, God gave Adam the task of giving names to all things animate and inanimate. As interpreted by Milton in *Paradise Lost*, Adam—in his innocence, in the state of grace he lived in before he came to know good and evil and was expelled from the Garden—is able to reveal the essences of each thing or creature he names, to reveal the truth of the world through language. After the fall, words were severed from things, and language became a collection of arbitrary signs—no longer connected to God or a universal truth.

Needless to say, I have spent my whole life exploring and meditating on my own name, and my great hope is to be reborn as an American Indian. Paul: Latin for small, little. Auster: Latin for South Wind. South Wind: an old American euphemism for a rectal toot. I therefore shall return to this world bearing the proud and altogether appropriate name of Little Fart.

Write again soon.

Yours ever,

Paul

Paul Auster and J. M. Coetzee

Dear John,

Just back from Ireland (yesterday) and the immense relief to have the "Beckett Address" behind me. A dinner with Edward Beckett, the nephew and executor, born 1943, a professional flautist and former music teacher, ensconced in London for many years, a shy, pleasant man, unsophisticated in literary matters, well meaning, earnest, more attached to his uncle as uncle than as literary hero. He was happy with my talk, said so several times, and that, finally, was all I was hoping to achieve: not to fall on my face in front of him and the other 500 people in the room. Gripped the podium tightly, my knees locked out of tension during the 50-minute discourse, and by the time I left the stage, my legs were so stiff I could barely move and nearly did—literally—fall on my face.

They plan to do this every year. I suggested you for the next one, and the organizers were enthusiastic. Perhaps you will hear from them in the coming months. It's your call, of course, whether to accept or not, but if you do accept, rest assured that you will be treated well.

While there, we learned that you are up for the Booker Prize. Fingers crossed on your behalf—and felicitations.

And then, this anguishing dilemma. We have been invited to a screening of *Disgrace* on the 17th—a film I am eager to see, in spite of your reservations—but it turns out that we have a conflict. A prior commitment, made many months ago, and when I suggested we break that date to attend the screening, Siri said she would never talk to me again, perhaps even kill me. I don't doubt that she means it. In today's *New York Times*,

Here and Now   85

however, which lists all the new films of the upcoming season, I see that the movie will be opening on Friday. We will go next weekend, then. Would you like me to clip local reviews for you—or would you rather not know?

With big hugs to you and Dorothy,

Paul

September 26, 2009

Dear Paul,

You write about the associations that the name "55th Street" has for you, and mention in passing Avenues A through Z in Manhattan. At once my thoughts go to the long poem of Galway Kinnell's on Avenue C. What a feat for a poet to have pulled off: a stranger from faraway Africa, hearing mention of avenues named after the letters of the alphabet, is at once transported (transpoeted, I nearly wrote) to the "God-forsaken avenue bearing the initial of Christ"!

I suppose that is one of the features that define a great city: with the passage of time, the names of its districts and quarters and streets and buildings become so woven into the tapestry of poems and stories that even readers who have never visited can find their way blindfolded: down 42nd Street as far as Baker Street, then make a left onto Nevsky Prospekt.

The 1950s and 1960s now look to me like a great age in American poetry, after which things have quietly gone downhill. Am I wrong? Is there something I am missing?

Rationalists are exasperated by the way in which words, even freshly minted ones, pick up connotations that blur their sharp denotative edges. One of the great projects of the Royal Society, founded in England in the late seventeenth century, was to establish a language free of associations, a language fit to be used by philosophers and scientists. The language that the scientific heirs of the Royal Society use today looks to us fairly pure, but only because it is based so heavily on Greek words, whose connotations are thoroughly lost to us (*electricity* from *elektron*, but who can say what this word, which denoted a precious-metal alloy, called up in the mind of Odysseus?).

(And what of my own response to *electric*, forever corrupted by the passage of "doom's electric moccasin"—Emily Dickinson?)

Though Swift made fun of the Royal Society project, the ideal it reached for was not ignoble. I have never fully understood why Beckett dropped English, but I suspect that part of the reason was that he found the language too encumbered with literary associations. Conrad, as I recall, inveighed against the English word *oak*, which, he said, could not be employed without evoking a whole history of British navigation and British empire.

It is not uncommon for writers, as they age, to get impatient with the so-called poetry of language and go for a more stripped-down style ("late style"). The most notorious instance, I suppose, is Tolstoy, who in later life expressed a moralistic disapproval of the seductive powers of art and confined himself to stories that would not be out of place in an elementary classroom. A loftier example is provided by Bach, who at the time of his death was working on his *Art of Fugue*, pure music in the sense that it is not tied to any particular instrument.

One can think of a life in art, schematically, in two or perhaps three stages. In the first you find, or pose for yourself, a great question. In the second you labor away at answering it. And then, if you live long enough, you come to the third stage, when the aforesaid great question begins to bore you, and you need to look elsewhere.

All the best,

John

Dear John,

We walked into the film with such low expectations (not only because of your remarks but because translating novels into movies is such a precarious business) and walked out pleasantly surprised, feeling the result wasn't half bad at all. Yes, John M. was miscast, but his performance was more subtle and less mannered than most of the things I've seen him in over the past few years—good enough, in any case, not to destroy the mood of the story. We thought the daughter was excellent—much thinner and more attractive than the character in the book, of course, but this is the movies, and what can you do, since attractive women are what the movies are all about. Direction, photography, production design, locations—admirably done. The New York reviews that I saw were largely favorable. The audience sitting in the theater with us was engrossed, and given how poor most films are these days, it was refreshing to see something with some spine and intelligence to it. No, it doesn't have the force of the book, but it tries to do justice to the book, and if I were in your shoes, I would feel reasonably satisfied, not the least bit betrayed. To add to your collection of UNIMPORTANT OBJECTS, I enclose our ticket stubs from the Quad Theater on 13th Street between 5th and 6th Avenues—just in case you want to show them off to your friends.

You talk about a golden age of American poetry in the fifties and sixties and then a quiet falling off. My first response was to say "nonsense," but now that I've given the matter some thought, I sadly have to admit that I agree with you. Most of the great modernists were still breathing then (Stevens died in 1954, but Pound, Eliot, and Williams all lived on into the sixties, Williams in particular doing some of his best work then), the so-called Objectivists were still thriving (the next generation, including Zukofsky, Oppen, and Reznikoff), Charles Olson was in full flower (how I loved Olson when I was young), and the generation after that (poets born in the 1920s) was emerging: Kinnell, whom you mention, but also Creeley, Ashbery, O'Hara, Merwin, Spicer, Ginsberg, and numerous others. Kinnell, Ashbery, and Merwin are still with us, but they are old men now, and what has happened after them? There are several poets born in the late thirties and early forties whose work I greatly admire and follow avidly—Michael Palmer (published by New Directions), Charles Simic (Harcourt), Ron Padgett (Coffee House Press) among them—not to speak of the somewhat younger Paul Muldoon (born in Northern Ireland, now an American citizen)—but they are all friends of mine, I have watched their work evolve over decades, and perhaps this personal connection clouds my judgment. I would be curious to know what you think of them, any one of them. There is also Susan Howe (New Directions), much admired, much debated, but oddly enough, the book I consider to be her best is a work of prose, *My Emily Dickinson*, an astonishingly brilliant and original text—in the spirit of Olson's *Call Me Ishmael* or Williams's *In the American Grain*: the poet as critic, criticism as a form of poetry, wonderful stuff. But no, none of these writers is as strong as the giants from the recent past. We live in an age of endless writing workshops, graduate writing programs (imagine getting a degree in writing), there are more poets per square inch than over before, more poetry magazines, more books of poetry (99% of them published by microscopic small presses), poetry slams, performance poets, cowboy poets—and yet, for all this activity, little of note is being written. The burning ideas that fueled the innovations of the early modernists seem to have been extinguished. No one believes that poetry (or art) can change the world anymore. No one is on a holy mission. Poets are everywhere now, but they talk only to each other.

Your reference to "late style" reminded me that I still haven't read Edward Said's book. I will try to track it down in the coming days. Tolstoy is a good example, but what about Joyce? It seems to me that his early style is late (by your definition, or by Said's definition) and that as he progressed from book to book he became more and more ornate, complex, baroque, culminating in a final book that is so complex that no one can read it (alas). But Joyce died at fifty-nine, and perhaps it could be argued that he didn't live long enough to have entered his late period. In any case, his is the only name that jumps out at me to contradict this theory. No, perhaps Henry James as well, whose final, dictated books are filled with some of the most tortuous sentences in English literature. Other writers, perhaps most writers, strike me as fairly consistent from beginning to end—Fielding, Dickens, Nabokov, Conrad, Roth, Updike, fill in the blanks. Not Beckett, of course, and in parallel with the late Bach, think of the late Matisse and his spare and sinuous cutouts. More stripped down, less stripped down, the same. Those are the three possibilities—which is to say, each person follows his or her own path. Goya said: "There are no rules in painting." Are there any rules in the life of an artist?

Summer seems to be over. Brisk days now, a new bite in the air. Siri plunges on with her novel, and I am unemployed again.

Warmest thoughts,

Paul

Paul Auster and J. M. Coetzee

Dear John,

I forgot to mention Robert Lowell. I forgot Elizabeth Bishop. I forgot John Berryman. I forgot Sylvia Plath. I forgot Robert Duncan. I forgot James Wright. I forgot William Bronk. I forgot Larry Eigner. I forgot H. D. (d. 1961) and Mina Loy (d. 1966) and Marianne Moore (d. 1972) and Laura Riding (d. 1991) and Lorine Niedecker (d. 1970). Not to speak of Theodore Roethke, Muriel Rukeyser, Denise Levertov, James Schuyler, Richard Wilbur, Barbara Guest, Kenneth Koch, and James Merrill. No doubt I am forgetting others still.

Yesterday, I bought Edward Said's *On Late Style*. Have read the first essay (mostly about Beethoven and Adorno) and see that the argument is not quite as simple as I originally thought. I will push on and give you my comments later.

Said, by the way, was the adviser for my M.A. thesis at Columbia in 1969–70—and we stayed in touch, off and on but warmly, until his death. The man who put the book together, Michael Wood, was another teacher of mine—and is still a friend. Just yesterday, Siri saw him at Princeton (where he now teaches) to talk to his class on the contemporary novel. I myself will be going to the same class in two weeks. I don't know why I mention this—simply because, I suppose, so many memories came rushing back to me when I bought the book yesterday.

All good thoughts—

Paul

October 9, 2009

Paul,

See below.
What does one do?
John

"22 September 2009

"J.M. Coetzee, c/o Vintage Books

"Dear Mr. Coetzee,

"I am disappointed and find it a shame that a writer enjoying such eminence as you do, should stoop to using anti-Semitic slurs, and these wholly gratuitously.

"I refer to your book 'Slow Man' Chapter 22 pages 167 and 168. Your reference to 'Jews' made in this derogatory way in no way furthered the story, and in my opinion should not have been used.

"For me an interesting book has been spoiled.

"Yours sincerely,

"[Name and address supplied]"

Dear John,

What to do? Do nothing—or something. That is to say, ignore the stupid letter and think no more about it. Or else, if you find yourself so deeply irked that it is impossible to stop thinking about it, write to the woman in England and tell her that you have written a novel, not a tract on ethical conduct, and that disparaging remarks about Jews, not to speak of out-and-out anti-Semitism, are a part of the world we live in, and just because your character says what she says does not mean that you endorse her comments. Lesson one in How to Read a Novel. Do writers of murder stories endorse murder? Do you, as a committed vegetarian, expose yourself as a hypocrite if one of your characters eats a hamburger? The woman's letter is absurd, idiotic. But the sad truth is that all novelists receive letters of this sort from time to time. My standard response is to crumple them up and toss them in the trash.

I imagine you have received my last letter by now, along with the card listing the names of more poets (still more, many more, have since occurred to me). I would appreciate your thoughts on the Adorno/Said notion of late style which, I confess, eludes me somewhat.

Hoping you are well.

Affectionately,

Paul

October 14, 2009

Dear Paul,

Last week I sent you a copy of a letter I had received from a reader in England, with a rather despairing accompanying note: What is one to do about this?

The letter points to a passage in my novel *Slow Man* in which Marijana Jokić, the Croatian inamorata of the hero, makes an anti-Semitic remark about a certain shopkeeper. The letter writer accuses me, as author of the book, of anti-Semitism.

You wrote back pointing out, very sensibly, that there are indeed things one can "do" about such a letter. One can ignore it, for instance. Or one can write back explaining that characters in novels have a degree of independence from their authors, and—particularly in the case of secondary characters—do not unfailingly speak for them.

You also point out that as a writer of a certain prominence I must expect to get all kinds of mail from readers, including mail that doesn't necessarily reflect a sophisticated understanding of what fiction is or does.

Yet my question still stands: What is one to do about this? For—the world being as it is, and the twentieth century in particular being what it was—an accusation of anti-Semitism, like an accusation of racism, throws one onto the defensive. "But I'm not one of them!" one wants to exclaim, displaying one's hands, showing that one's hands are clean.

The real question, however, is not whose hands are clean and whose are not. The real question arises out of the moment of being thrown onto the defensive, and out of the sinking feel-

Paul Auster and J. M. Coetzee

ing that comes next, the feeling that the goodwill between reader and writer has evaporated, the goodwill without which reading loses its joy and writing begins to feel like an unwanted, burdensome exercise. What does one do after *that*? Why go on, when one's words are being picked over for covert slights and heresies? It's like being back among the Puritans.

Enough of that. You ask what I make of Edward Said, your old teacher, on the subject of late style. I confess I don't remember much of what he has to say, except that I found myself adhering stubbornly to the old-fashioned understanding of late style that he was engaged in attacking. In the case of literature, late style, to me, starts with an ideal of a simple, subdued, unornamented language and a concentration on questions of real import, even questions of life and death. Of course once you get beyond that starting point the writing itself takes over and leads you where it will. What you end up with may be anything but simple, anything but subdued.

In your last letter you go through a roll call of postwar American poets, poets who made their mark after 1945, and really it is a very distinguished list. Do we see their like today? I suppose I should be cautious about coming out with too quick a reply: the old are notoriously blind to the virtues of the young. But I will say that among today's readers I see very few who take their lead in life from what the poets of our day are saying. Whereas I do believe that in the 1960s and, up to a point, the 1970s a lot of young people—indeed, many of the best young people—took poetry as the truest guide to living there was. I am referring here to young people in the United States, but the same held for Europe—in fact, most strongly of all for Eastern Europe. Who today has the power to shape young souls that Brodsky or Herbert or Enzensberger or (in a more dubious way) Allen Ginsberg had?

Something happened, it seems to me, in the late 1970s or early 1980s as a result of which the arts yielded up their leading role in our inner life. I am quite prepared to give heed to diagnoses of what happened between then and now that have a political or economic or even world-historical character; but I do nevertheless feel that there was a general failure among writers and artists to resist the challenge to their leading role, and that we are poorer today for that failure.

All the best,

John

Dear John,

Just to cheer you up for a moment (if cheer is the proper word to use in this context). The other night, I participated in a PEN-sponsored event called "Reckoning with Torture," which documented the abuses of the U.S. government under Bush (cover page of the program is enclosed), and in his opening remarks, Anthony Appiah, the new president of American PEN, cited a passage from *Diary of a Bad Year*—the one about Sibelius and Guantánamo, about pride in humanity and shame in humanity—and it made me glad (if glad is the proper word to use in this context) to know that you were among us that night and to be given proof that people exist out there who are fully engaged in your work—as opposed, say, to the English woman whose letter so deeply and justifiably upset you.

Forgive me for being so slow in answering your last fax—dated nine days ago. The truth is that I have been struggling to say something pertinent in response to your remark about the arts playing a diminished role in our inner life since the late seventies or early eighties. I have filled several pages with my rants and opinions, but they don't satisfy me. I find them shallow and boring, and I hesitate to inflict them on you. Also: the more I have pondered the question, the more depressed I have become—overwhelmed by a feeling that I have been writing an obituary of my own time, my own life.

Some of the approaches I have attempted are: 1) an analysis of capitalism triumphant; 2) the victory of pop culture over "high" culture; 3) the collapse of Communism, and with it the collapse of revolutionary idealism, the notion that society can be reinvented; 4) the death of modernism.

Answers might be found in exploring these subjects, but all I have found is sadness.

But you are right. Something is gone now that used to be there. I don't know if artists themselves are to be blamed for this loss. There are probably too many factors involved to blame anyone in particular. One thing is certain, however: stupidity has increased on all fronts. If one reads the letters of soldiers from the American Civil War, many of them turn out to be more literate, more articulate, more sensitive to the nuances of language than the writing of most English professors today. Bad schools? Bad governments that allow bad schools to exist? Or simply too many distractions, too many neon lights, too many computer screens, too much noise?

My only consolation is that art forges on, in spite of everything. It is an unquenchable human need, and even in these grim times, there are countless numbers of good writers and artists, even great writers and artists, and even if the audience for their work has grown smaller, there are still enough people who care about art and literature to make the pursuit worthwhile.

I'm sorry to have given you so little today. I am in a funk. I will do better next time, I promise.

With great affection,

Paul

Dear Paul,

May I return briefly to our discussion of sport?

I've been reading a book about the history of quantification, *Trust in Numbers* by Theodore M. Porter (1995). Porter is concerned to show that our passion for the figures in "facts and figures" is of fairly recent origin: he dates the stirrings of the quantificatory spirit to the mid–eighteenth century

It occurs to me that the rise of mass sports and the cult of numbers may be not unconnected; in other words, that there may be a reason why sports are delivered to us nowadays in numerical packaging.

Take the various football codes as an example. As far as I know, the progenitor of football, in Europe, was an annual tussle between the young men of neighboring villages to secure a nominated trophy and bring it home. The form of the trophy didn't really matter. It may once have been a head, human or animal, but usually it was a bladder or ball. There were very few rules ("teams" were of any size, the field was the whole countryside, the competition was in running and/or blocking and/or wrestling, probably in eye-gouging too), and the game ended when, in effect, the first goal was scored.

It was only in the mid–nineteenth century that rules of such contests were codified to make it a proper game. It was with this codification that the game began to take on its present numerical cast: number of players, size and marking of field, length of game, criteria for goal scoring, definition of victory, etc.

Or consider bat-and-ball games. I take these to have their

origin in a form of play in which one man hurls stones at another man, who defends himself with a shield or stick. This play becomes less dangerous when the target is redefined (in cricket) as an object which the man with the stick defends, and further redefined (in baseball) as an abstract torso-sized target more or less behind the man with the stick. What the reformers do with the resulting game is to add a heavy numerical overlay—distance between the two men, size and composition of "ball" (stone), size of "bat" (stick), etc.—and then to superadd a whole new system of abstract numerical rewards for hitting the ball (runs) and penalties for quitting your "at bat" post, etc.

It is only once the primitive contests have been thus reconceived as rule-governed recreations, and victory has been given an abstract, numerical definition, that they are welcomed into modern life.

Boxing is an interesting case. It remains the closest in spirit to the primitive contest. Though the quantifiers have done their best to modernize it (awarding points for blows, for example, at least in the amateur code), it remains only partly tamed, and thus hovers somewhat on the fringes of polite sport.

It further occurs to me that a certain kind of male child is drawn to sports like baseball and cricket because they combine the hero worship common to all sport ("I wish my father were like X!" with the variant "The man who calls himself my father is not my real father; my real father is X") with the socially sanctioned systems of quantification that allow quick but immature minds to evade difficult questions like, "Are the men who call themselves Team A better than the men who call themselves Team B?" or "Is there a way in which the communal virtue of Team A may exceed the sum of the virtues of its individual members?"

These reflections were sparked by reading the interview you recently gave Kevin Rabalais (it appeared in last weekend's *Australian* newspaper), which included a cautionary tale of what can happen to a boy who doesn't take care to have his pencil ready at all times.

Thanks for your letter of October 23. I can offer no better an answer than you to the question of why artists were important to our lives fifty years ago but are no longer so.

As regards your sense that you are and perhaps have for a while been writing an obituary of your own times and your own life, let me mention that I recently heard about a burgeoning field in terminal care: the dying person is assisted by a professionally trained counselor to record their reflections on their own life—achievements, regrets, reminiscences, the works—which are then tastefully packaged (CD, bound printout) and passed on to the surviving family. It has been shown, said the promoter of the concept, that having a chance to tell their story in this way enables patients to die more peacefully.

All the best,

John

Dear John,

The day after sending off my last letter to you, I received the manuscript of the English-language translation of a novel written by a friend of mine—a great mountain of a book, three or four times longer than anything either one of us has ever written. The translator is someone new to him (his previous translator has retired), and because my friend considers this to be his most important book (it is), and because his grasp of English is shaky, I offered some months ago to read the translation and give comments to his American editor. I finished the job yesterday—a slow, painstaking slog through thousands and thousands of sentences, puzzled from beginning to end by the translator's numerous errors, slowly coming to the conclusion (not yet confirmed) that English is not her first language. The mistakes are mostly small ones—"like" for "as if," "me and him" for "he and I," split infinitives, adjectives used as adverbs, and a maddening confusion between transitive and intransitive verbs—but the cumulative effect is jarring, making the book unpublishable as it stands now. Corrections will be made, of course, everything will come out right in the end, but all through my labors I kept thinking back to our discussion several months ago about the notion of a "mother tongue" and how truly complex a business it is to master a language, how many rules and principles and exceptions to rules and principles must be absorbed into one's bloodstream to be able to "own" a particular idiom. The slightest misstep reveals a failure to understand how the system works. A single flub, and alarm bells start ringing. Not unlike what happened to me the other day when I called our local car service for a ride into Manhattan. I gave the female dispatcher the address, which she must have looked up on a computer map, and then she asked me if it was between such-and-such street and Houston Street (pronouncing it Hewston, like the city in Texas). Everyone who lives in New York knows that it is pronounced Howston—and I immediately said to her: "You're not from New York, are you?" and she said no, she had in fact just moved here. It reminded me of certain scenes in war movies, spy movies, in which a German posing as an American or an American posing as a German gives himself away with a small slip like that—saying Hewston instead of Howston and thus exposing himself as an impostor. The firing squad comes next. A whole battalion is slaughtered. The war is lost. How intricate the knowledge of a mother tongue, how subtle its workings!

Your insight into the Enlightenment's mania for quantification and the development of organized sports is ingenious. I don't know how familiar you are with baseball, but given the time you have spent in America, you must have at least a passing acquaintance with it. As you are probably aware, it is a sport dominated by numbers. Every play, every action within a play is immediately transformed into a statistic, and since those statistics are kept on file, every action that takes place in a game today is read in the context of the entire history of the sport. Few Americans can remember who the president was in 1927, but anyone who follows baseball will be able to tell you that 1927 was the year Babe Ruth hit sixty home runs. To give you a taste of this almost Talmudic obsession with numbers, I enclose a photocopy of a page from *The Baseball Encyclopedia* which, among other things, includes the career record of every player who has participated in even a single game since the sport was invented. Note that Paddy Mayes's entire career consisted of just five games, all in 1911, whereas Willie Mays, the legendary Willie Mays (he of the absent pencil story), played from 1951 to 1973 and appeared in 2,992 games. Quantification indeed. To the uninitiated, these charts will look like utter nonsense.

•

You mention that the rules of football were codified in the mid–nineteenth century. While researching my little piece on soccer/football more than ten years ago, I found out that standard rules were introduced as early as 1801—even closer to the mid–eighteenth century and the birth of the "quantificatory spirit," thus making it possible for Napoleon to have been defeated "on the playing fields of Eton." But you are right about the *present-day* rules of football, which were drawn up at Cambridge University in 1863.

As for bat-and-ball games, I stumbled across this theory about the origins of cricket: knocking down three-legged milkmaid stools with a thrown object (stone? ball?) and then, as time went on, to make the game more challenging, the introduction of a stick to prevent the object from hitting the stool. The three legs of the stool eventually became the wicket. Plausible? Perhaps.

•

You refer to the interview I did with Kevin Rabalais for *The Australian*. To tell the truth, I have absolutely no memory of what I said to him. Nor can I remember anything I have ever said to any interviewer over the years. Hundreds of conversations of which not a single syllable remains. And yet, with so-called normal conversations, that is, with Siri, with you, with any of my friends or associates or relatives, I am usually able to recall most of what was said. Is an interview somehow a non-event, an abnormal event, a conversation that is not a conversation? Even during the course of an interview, I tend to forget what I have just said. The words leave my mouth and then vanish forever. Is it the pressure to answer the question now before me that makes me forget the previous one? Does the fear of saying something stupid inhibit my capacity to remember? Is it the tedium of talking about myself?

When you were here last summer, you mentioned that you have stopped giving interviews. But did something similar ever happen to you in the past—or am I the only one afflicted by this peculiar form of amnesia?

In any case, if I told Kevin Rabalais the story about the pencil, I must have been talking about my encounter with Willie Mays when I was eight years old. Did I go on to recount the postscript—something that happened less than three years ago? If not, let me know, and I will share it with you in my next letter, since it is a strange and moving story, one worth telling.

•

On the subject of memory, something happened to us last night that has left us both rather stunned. About twenty-five years ago, Siri and I saw a film on the public television channel, an obscure 1933 Depression comedy-drama starring Claudette Colbert, *Three-Cornered Moon*. We both thought it was terrifically well done, and for the past quarter century we have referred to it as a lost treasure, one of the best movies of the period. Last week, I discovered that the film has been released on DVD and ordered a copy—which arrived yesterday. We eagerly put it on after dinner, and then, much to our disappointment, our separate and mutual disappointment, discovered that it is not a very good film at all, mediocre at best. How could we have been so mistaken in our judgment? Even more important, we had both misremembered essential aspects of the plot—but in different ways. Siri thought Claudette Colbert had three sisters, when in fact she has three brothers. I thought Claudette Colbert had saved the family from ruin by going out and getting herself a job, when in fact she loses her job after just two weeks.

What to make of this?

It strikes me that memory might be something we could investigate. Or, if that is too vast a subject, the deceptions of memory.

    With warmest thoughts,

    Paul

November 22, 2009

Dear John,

This, from the sports section of today's Sunday *Times*, which might amuse you (on the heels of your last letter), especially the statement: "the future of the game is in the numbers." The statistics they are talking about here go far beneath—or beyond—the charts I sent you the other day. We are coming closer and closer to a realm of pure theoretical physics.

On the other hand, even if everything they do can be translated into numbers, the players themselves are not robots. Witness the lovely 1946 photo of Ted Williams and Stan Musial—two of the all-time greats.

Thinking of you . . .

All best,

Paul

Dear Paul,

You ask whether I have had the experience of giving an interview and then being unable to remember what I had said. Not exactly. But I have often felt oppressive boredom as I listen to myself mouthing off to interviewers. To my way of thinking, real talk only occurs when there is some kind of current running between the interlocutors. And such a current rarely runs during interviews.

I'll be glad to discuss memory with you at some time in the future, if we can remember to get back to it. At present the aspect of memory that concerns me most is absentmindedness. I watch myself with a hawk's eye for the first sign, as the end of my seventieth decade on earth approaches, that my mind is going. No sign yet—at least, no sign that I will admit to be a sign.

Thanks for the pages of baseball statistics. They are all too reminiscent of the pages of the *Cricketers' Almanack*, otherwise known as Wisden's, which collects the world's cricket statistics year by year.

I have been thinking about food—food and food taboos. I have been aware for a long time that Franz Kafka was a vegetarian. More recently I learned that this caused much dissension in the parental home—dissension that Kafka himself was perhaps not averse to fomenting. Now I have come across Ernst Pawel's book on Kafka.* Pawel takes Kafka's attitude to food seriously, as I suppose anyone must who has read "The

* Ernst Pawel, *The Nightmare of Reason: A Life of Franz Kafka* (New York: Farrar Straus Giroux, 1984).

Hunger Artist." Kafka, says Pawel, drew unconsciously upon Jewish dietary law to create for himself a set of rituals of an ascetic, self-punishing, and finally destructive nature. One consequence of adhering to these rituals was that he gradually alienated himself from his family, to the point where he began to take his meals by himself.

It seems to me that there are two discourses of food going on around us, and they have surprisingly little contact with each other. The one is the discourse of dining and cuisine, which has expanded massively to the point where there are entire magazines devoted to it. The other is a discourse of eating pathology, covering psychophysical afflictions like anorexia and bulimia, and more generally the spread of obesity.

The question that pesters me is the following. Is it really so that there is a minority of the population (though perhaps in some countries a disturbingly large minority) who, to use the current euphemism, "have issues," as Kafka did, with food, as opposed to a majority in whose lives food has no particularly deep meaning, to whom it is bodily nourishment and maybe a source of transitory pleasure, but nothing more? Might dividing people up into these two crude classes not be akin to dividing people up into those who "have issues" with their parents and those who have none? Don't we all "have issues" with our parents, only of different kinds and in different degrees? (I pose these questions with the spirit of Freud hovering at my elbow.) How many of us would get a clean bill of health from a Pawel-like investigator?

We like to think that there was a time—not too long ago—when food was so scarce that only a privileged few could afford to pick and choose, and therefore to "have issues." To the hoi polloi, who presumably included your ancestors and mine, getting enough to eat was the only thing that mattered; if by good fortune you managed to put on a little weight, that was a cause of self-congratulation on your part and of envy on the part of your neighbors.

In this version of social history, it can only be recently—let us say in the past fifty or a hundred years—that troubled relations with the food we eat or don't eat can have developed on a large scale.

But I wonder whether this version is true. I wonder whether, even in conditions of scarcity, it is not possible to have troubled relations with food. What, after all, is the phenomenon of the fast, enjoined by all religions, all about? (I mean, what is it about in terms other than the terms provided by the religions themselves, like purification of the spirit, mortification of the flesh, etc?) It is not as though the question of whether even the poor and illiterate have troubled relations with food is unanswerable: there are billions of people all around the world living in conditions of scarcity—we have merely to ask them. But is anyone exploring the deeper meanings of food in their lives? Not that I am aware of.

There is a passing remark of Freud's that I find relevant here. What distinguishes the erotic life of the ancients from erotic life today, Freud said, is that in ancient times the focus of attention was on the erotic impulse, whereas today it is on the erotic object. Apply this to food writing. What would it mean to shift one's attention from the comparative attractions of X and Y on the menu to the question of what it is in me that leads me to choose X over Y? Is it really true that gustatorial pleasure is unanalyzable, that it has no history, that it has no psychic dimension (no psychic dimension in the life of the individual subject)? Do we really accept that there should be a ban on such analysis (a spoilsport ban)?

One of the explanations for food taboos put forward by anthropologists is that the taboo defines an in-group as against an out-group, and is thus a kind of glue holding the in-group together. In this explanation, the content of the taboo is of secondary importance (marine animals that lack scales; cow's milk). But this feels to me excessively abstract. A Westerner who sees an unfamiliar-looking carcass hanging in a Vietnamese roadside stall, and asks what it is, and is told it is a dog, feels a moment of authentic revulsion, I would guess, even nausea. To be told that his revulsion is culturally conditioned doesn't mitigate it. The Vietnamese around him, smiling and joking about his reaction, don't seem any the less—what is the word?—odious.

Go back to Franz Kafka at the table of Hermann Kafka. We have an idea, thanks to Pawel, of how Franz must have seemed to a sensible bourgeois like Hermann; but how did Hermann seem to Franz?

All the best,

John

Dear John,

I laughed out loud when I read about your willingness to discuss memory with me "some time in the future, if we can remember to get back to it." In the next sentence of your letter, you refer to absentmindedness, and then, in the next sentence after that, you say that you are approaching the end of your seventieth *decade* on earth—which would mean that you are seven hundred years old! A slip, of course, the kind of thing we all do from time to time, even when we are young, even when we are not generally prone to absentmindedness, but somehow hilarious when the slip occurs during a discussion of absent-mindedness.

For a man of your advanced years, I must say that you were looking remarkably fit the last time I saw you.

.

I'm sure you remember the Russian film we all liked so much at the festival last year, *Wild Field*. It still has no distributor in the U.S., and because that strikes me as an injustice, I recently called an acquaintance of mine, a curator in the film department at the Museum of Modern Art (one of the people responsible for selecting the lineup for the New Directors/New Films Festival held there every spring), and invited him to our house to watch the DVD. He responded enthusiastically and said he would do everything in his power to get the film shown. Excellent news. Then, the very next day, he called to tell me that one of his colleagues in the film department is currently in Georgia (the country, not the state) to organize a festival of

Georgian cinema for the museum and that she, too, had just seen *Wild Field* and was similarly impressed and enthusiastic. More good news, yes, but then the other shoe dropped. It seems that the director—the same forty-nine-year-old man we met in Estoril who was so articulate and charming during the Q. and A. that followed the screening of his film—died less than a month ago. My friend couldn't give me any details. So sad. The last thing in the world I was expecting to hear. I thought you and Dorothy should know. . . .

In your last letter, you mentioned the interview I did with *The Australian* and the story about the pencil I couldn't remember having told the journalist. I promised to give you the sequel if I hadn't already done so. Since you didn't mention it in your new letter, I assume I haven't.

The first part is printed on pages 271–272 of my *Collected Prose*—section 5 of a sequence of true stories, *Why Write?* Once you have absorbed that moment of childhood misery, now this:

In January 2007, Siri and I escaped the cold of New York to attend a literary festival in Key West, Florida. One of the writers there was Amy Tan, whom I had met a couple of times back in the nineties through a mutual friend, film director Wayne Wang. Years earlier, Wayne had told me an interesting story about Amy, which I included in another sequence of true stories, *Accident Report* (page 273 of *Collected Prose*). Seeing Amy again, I realized that I had forgotten to send her a copy of the book in which the story had been published—so I bought one for her in Key West. She read the story about herself on the plane back home to San Francisco—as well as all the other stories in the book, including the one about Willie Mays. It turned out that the then seventy-six-year-old retired baseball player lived in a town near San Francisco and that two of Amy's friends happened to be his next-door neighbors. Amy called them immediately after she walked into her house, told them to go out and buy a copy of my book, and then knock on Willie Mays's door and read him the story I had written about our encounter in 1955. According to Amy's friends, Willie's eyes teared up as he listened to the story, and then for a minute or two afterward he just sat there shaking his head, repeating over and over again, "Fifty-two years, fifty-two years . . ."

Amy called Siri to tell her about this, but I was kept in the dark. The following week, which happened to be the week of my sixtieth birthday, kind Amy Tan came to New York, invited us to dinner, and presented me with a baseball autographed by Willie Mays. The old man finally got what the little boy had so desperately wanted. He no longer wanted it, of course, but that was beside the point. If nothing else, he was moved by the fact that Willie was moved.

•

I hesitate to impose more of my old pieces on you, but if you do in fact have *Collected Prose* at hand, you might want to take a look at *Pages for Kafka* (page 303), *The Art of Hunger* (317), and *New York Babel* (325). These are ancient texts, all written when I was in my twenties, but they are directly linked to some of the questions you raise concerning Kafka and food.

I remember buying the Pawel book when it was first published (1984!—it doesn't seem possible that so much time has passed) and thinking that it was by far the best work on Kafka I had read. I doubt that any subsequent biography has surpassed it. The passage you refer to is both chilling and insightful, a dissection of the same compulsion for self-sabotage I tried to evoke in my short, highly abstract young man's piece. Kafka is an extreme example of food torment, but I agree with you that nearly all of us have "issues" with food, not necessarily the eating pathologies you refer to, but, let us say, "complicated relations" with what we put in our mouths. For the same reason you cite when referring to Freud: there is surely a psychological component that would explain why we are attracted to X on the menu and not Y. Does it all go back to buried memories from childhood? Probably.

I found all your points well taken, am not inclined to dispute any of them, but we might want to consider the social function of food, the rituals of feast days (the same dishes served every year at Christmas, Thanksgiving, Passover), the very concept of a meal itself. Why not simply eat when we are hungry, when our stomach tells us to eat? Who commanded that the day be divided into breakfast, lunch, and dinner? Reading about Kafka's habit of eating alone, it struck me that most of us do not like to eat alone, that nearly everyone eats with others (couples, friends, families, children in school cafeterias) and that meals are generally an occasion for talk. Food goes into your mouth, words come out of it.

For the first half of my life, I had little truck with ceremonies of any kind. Birthday celebrations, national and religious holidays, anniversary parties—they all left me cold, and I shunned them as best I could. Then, twenty-nine years ago, I tiptoed my way into the Hustvedt clan and discovered the intricate protocols of Norwegian Christmas. Siri and her three sisters are all serious, free-thinking, secular people, and yet, under the guidance of their equally secular parents, the six of them demonstrated an absolute, unswerving faith in the importance of upholding this tradition. There is the tree, of course, and the giving of presents, but the heart of the tradition is the Christmas dinner—which never changes. Every item on the menu is exactly the same from year to year, ending with a dessert of rice pudding topped with raspberry sauce, one helping of which always contains a "magic" almond (put in there by Siri's mother): the person with the almond in his or her bowl is given a prize, which turns out to be more food: a large tablet of chocolate.

The first time I attended one of these Christmas dinners, I didn't know what to think. It struck me as absurd that six intelligent people would engage in such childish rituals, but at the same time the happiness and solidarity among the six participants was impressive. No family in my experience had ever seemed more harmonious, more closely knit.

As the years passed, the clan grew. Each sister married and had children, and by the time the family had attained its peak population (before the death of Siri's father), there were nineteen people sitting around the table for Christmas dinner. The new generation has embraced the tradition with the same enthusiasm as the elders, and not one child has ever complained about having to eat the same food every year. The repetition of the menu seems to give everyone comfort, and with another Christmas looming up next week, I confess that I, the old skeptic of yore, am looking forward to it.

Paul Auster and J. M. Coetzee

Thank you for the kind words you e-mailed to Siri about the Woodian attack on my work, my life, and whatever it is I seem to represent for him. I haven't read it. I have stopped reading all reviews of my books, whether good or bad, but I heard enough from others about what he wrote to feel as if I had been mugged by a stranger. If you are punched, your impulse is to punch back. In this situation, that isn't allowed—which is exceedingly frustrating—but the sting has lessened with the passing of time. Otherwise, according to my editor, Frances Coady, whom you met in Australia in '08 (Peter Carey's wife), response has been uniformly positive and they are about to re-print the book for the fourth time in six weeks. So I mustn't complain, least of all about a man whose name suggests that one day he will be eaten by termites.

With a hearty Ho Ho Ho,

Paul

Dear Paul,

The picture you evoke of meals in the Hustvedt household is most interesting.

In the paradigmatic version of the family table there seem to be three stages. In the first you graduate from infanthood to a place at the table, where you spend some years cautiously observing how people older than yourself conduct themselves. In the second you begin to rebel against the order of the table, against "table manners," which now seem to you to embody everything that is false and hypocritical about society and the family in particular. Your rebellion may proceed to the point where you take your plate of food to your bedroom and eat it there, or else sneak food from the refrigerator. Then in the third stage—the stage you describe—you rediscover the table as a site of integration, and even begin to assert the values of the table against rebellious younger participants.

What interest me are the customs that have developed around the table. Thus, despite the fact that the table is precisely a place to which one brings one's animal appetites in order to satisfy them, manners prescribe that appetite should be reined in and—at least formally—yield place to the appetites of others ("Please, after you!"). Furthermore, it is not "good manners" to sate one's appetite in silence: the dinner table becomes a sort of conclave where family matters of the more superficial kind are aired. In these family conversations, the first rule is that the passions should not be let loose, however much they may rage under the surface. (This is of course what children approaching the age of rebellion find most insufferable about family meals: the playacting.)

There is perhaps a fourth stage to the paradigm. The children have flown the nest, father and mother are left facing each other across the table. Will they speak (obeying, however, the rule that proscribes passionate speech) or will they lapse into a silence that will extend itself, and harden, year after year?

I should mention that I too have been the object of the attentions of the critic you name. It's a peculiar position one finds oneself in. Quite aside from the question of animus on the critic's part, there may be errors of fact in the review, or elementary misreadings. Should one react? Should one write a letter to the editor, a rejoinder to the unfair review? It is not as if editors would not welcome such a response—there is nothing their readers relish more than a good literary spat in the correspondence columns.

The sage writer will be cautious here. He will know that to betray irritation, to say nothing of outrage or (God forbid!) hurt feelings, will be fatal: it will turn him into a figure of fun. Knowing this, the critic is further emboldened. He becomes like the child lobbing pebbles at the gorilla in the zoo, knowing he is protected by the bars.

All good wishes,

John

Dear John,

At Christmas dinner the other week, I asked the youngest members of the family (ages seven, ten, and fifteen) if they found it unpleasant to be forced to eat the same food every year—with no variations whatsoever—and they all said that they loved it, that the sameness was what made it so enjoyable, and that they looked forward to that dinner with great eagerness every year.

The consolations of ritual. A ritual in which religion plays no part. The consolations of family ritual.

Siri, who cooked the meal at our house, neglected to prepare one of the traditional offerings: boiled red cabbage—which, I would venture to say, no one in the Hustvedt clan eats except at Christmas. When the absence of the dish was finally noted, a general lamentation was heard around the table. Siri apologized for her forgetfulness and promised to be more attentive next year.

It would seem that every detail counts.

•

Critics. You are right: it would be fatal for a novelist to respond publicly to a malicious attack. In recent years, however, I've heard of two such incidents—neither one consisting of an exchange of letters. The eighty-year-old Norman Mailer punching a critic in the stomach for giving him a bad review. And Richard Ford spitting in the face of a younger novelist who had written a vile, mean-spirited article about his latest book. My sympathies were with the puncher and the spitter—probably because I myself am too well mannered to punch or spit, much as I have sometimes wanted to.

Twenty years ago, I had my chance, but I couldn't go through with it. A book critic from the *Los Angeles Times* (who had previously worked as a theater critic for the *New York Times*) wrote an extremely hostile review of *Moon Palace*. Not just a negative review, but an out-and-out assault. Roughly a year after that, the editor of the *New York Times* op-ed page commissioned me to write a Christmas story—my one and only commission, my one and only short story, which evolved into the film *Smoke* a few years later. It was the first work of fiction ever published in the *Times* (not counting the erroneous news stories they have printed, of course), and the editor was proud of himself for having thought of the idea, pleased with the results and the favorable comments from readers, and so he invited me out to lunch as a way of thanking me for my efforts. We went to a restaurant near the *Times* building, a place heavily frequented by *Times* employees, and when the lunch was over and we were about to leave, he spotted the reviewer from the *L.A. Times*, his former colleague in New York. "Look, there's X," he said. "Let's go over and say hello." I didn't have time to tell him that X had written a nasty review of my novel and that I had no desire to meet him. When the op-ed page editor announced my name to X, the man's face went white, and I saw fear in his eyes. He looked like someone who was expecting to be punched, and I confess that for a brief instant I felt tempted to oblige him. But only for an instant. It seemed far better to pretend that I had no idea who he was, had never heard of his name, had never read the review, and therefore I politely shook his hand and told him how happy I was to meet him. He looked both shocked and relieved—there would be no punch, after all—and for those few moments I felt a strange sense of power (never felt before, never felt since), knowing that I was in complete control of this man's fate, that he was utterly in my hands. I had behaved beautifully, I thought, and I left the restaurant basking in my moral triumph.

Now, I'm not so sure I did the right thing. Years passed, many years, and eventually X returned to the *New York Times* as an occasional reviewer of books. As I mentioned in my last letter, I have stopped reading reviews of my work, but last year (fall 2008) I opened my morning copy of the *Times* to read over breakfast, and there, to my surprise, was a review of *Man in the Dark* by X. No one had told me the review would be running that day, and with the piece directly before my eyes, my resolve weakened, and I read the article in spite of myself. Another blistering assault from the man I probably should have punched twenty years ago. One sentence has stuck with me and will never be expunged from my mind: "Paul Auster does not believe in traditional fictional values." What on earth does that mean? It sounds like something a right-wing politician might say during an election campaign.

Somewhere, somehow, I happened to learn that our birthdays fall during the same week. Mine is February third, and yours, I believe, is the ninth. If I am correct, then a significant milestone is looming in your immediate future, and I send you warmest good wishes from across the seas.

I suspect that you are not someone who cares much about these things, but I wonder if Dorothy is pushing you into some

Paul Auster and J. M. Coetzee

kind of celebration, or if you will allow the day to go by without any fuss. This is not a personal question. I'm interested in why some of us actively embrace celebrations and rituals (i.e., Siri and Christmas), and others of us do not.

We have been back from Spain and France for a few days now and have more or less readjusted to New York time. Very cold there, very cold here, and, it seems, very cold in parts of Australia as well. Already, I am longing for spring.

Best thoughts,

Paul

Dear Paul,

I know you are not an habitué of literary salons, but you do live in a cultural metropolis and are therefore fated to cross paths now and then with the folk who review your books. I, on the other hand, run little risk of meeting the sort of person who makes a living by saying clever things at other people's expense, and consequently, unlike you, I have never needed to restrain myself from punching one of them on the nose.

For someone as thin-skinned as myself, at least in my everyday dealings, I have always found it puzzling that I don't take bad reviews to heart. Puzzling, but not puzzling enough for me to want to find out why this is so, in case I should suddenly lose that useful carapace.

An incapacity to get upset by what other people say about me, and its obverse, an incapacity to sympathize thoroughly with people who do get upset, is, I suspect, the weakness at the heart of a book I published in 1996 under the title *Giving Offense*. Why be offended by insults to your religion (or your country or your race or your moral standards), I ask there — why not simply shrug them off and get on with your life?

The answer that many (most?) people would give is: Because I can't. Because my sense of myself is under attack. Because failing to take offense would leave me feeling humiliated.

I am sure that in rare cases there is a kernel of irreducible truth in a response like this. But my instinct, or my predilection, now and when I wrote *Giving Offense*, has been to treat such a response as a cover for a reactive impulse to which the offended party would be reluctant to confess: belligerence of spirit, an appetite for a good scrap.

One reason why I should be, or can afford to be, thick-skinned vis-à-vis reviewers is that I have never had to depend on my books for a livelihood. Until I retired from teaching not long ago, I had a perfectly adequate academic salary to depend on. I could have been panned by every critic on earth, my book sales could have plummeted to zero, and I would not have starved. The uglier side of Grub Street—the animosities, the fawning and backbiting, and so forth—comes from a some-times desperate need to scrounge a living.

Anyway, bravo to you for your forbearance, and boo to the critic in question for failing to be ennobled by your example.

Yes, I am seventy now—thank you for your good wishes. I'll look in the mirror, when I have a moment, to check whether I have entered upon the sixth or, *horribile dictu*, the seventh of the Shakespearean ages. I pray it is only the sixth, the age of the lean and slippered pantaloon with shrunken shanks and quavering voice, and not the last, the return to childishness, sans teeth etcetera.

Yours ever,

John

Dear John,

For reasons I can't quite grasp (possibly because you are so far away and our meetings are so infrequent), I often find myself wanting to *give you things*. The package of books last month, for example, and now the enclosed DVD of the Italian edition of *Man on Wire*. The film is about the same man, Philippe Petit, whose book I translated years ago and included in that package. I was interviewed for the DVD in a hotel lobby in Milan last year, and now I have been sent ten copies. With nine to spare, off one goes to you.

I don't know if you have already seen the film, which was released in 2008 and made something of a splash (Academy Award for best documentary), but if you haven't seen it, it's quite possible that you have no idea who Philippe Petit is. Most famously, he is the man who walked on a wire between the towers of the World Trade Center in 1974.

If you look at the interview I did for the DVD, you will learn of my connection to Philippe—so no need to rehash that here. There is also the essay I wrote in 1982 ("On the High Wire," in *Collected Prose*), which was supposed to serve as the introduction to the book I translated but—for highly strange and amusing reasons—never appeared in the volume.

The essay mentions the name of Cyrus Vance, who served as secretary of state under Jimmy Carter and who was present at one of Philippe's performances that I attended. I included Vance as a rhetorical point—to prove that high-wire walking is an entirely *democratic* art, able to excite the interest of all people, from young children to former secretaries of state. When I showed my piece to Philippe, however, he said—first—Who is Cyrus Vance?—and when I told him, he said—second—that he didn't want the name of a politician in his book. I was dumbfounded. Don't you understand? I said. I included him to make a point about what you do. No, no, Philippe replied, you have to cut out his name, I won't stand for it. Exasperated and incensed, I told him that he was an idiot, refused to delete the name, and withdrew my introduction.

A small but maddening example of Philippe's arrogance, self-importance, and single-minded, all-consuming vanity. Then again, without that personality, it is unimaginable that he ever would have tried to do what he did. Fortunately, the quarrel didn't last. We remained friends, and some years later, when I found him a French publisher for the same book, he was all too happy to have my introduction included.

All that is secondary, not the reason for this letter today. I am far more interested in what Philippe does—particularly the three walks documented in the film: Nôtre Dame in Paris, the Sydney Harbour Bridge, and the World Trade Center. I don't know how you will respond to these feats (or have responded to them), but for me they are among the most extraordinarily beautiful and thrilling accomplishments I have ever witnessed, acts of such stupefying grandeur that I tremble whenever I think about them.

In one of your earlier letters, you talked about watching Federer play tennis: "I have just seen something that is at the same time human and more than human; I have just seen something like the human ideal made visible." Then, a couple of paragraphs down, referring to masterworks of art: "Yet it was done by a man . . . like me; what an honor to belong to the species that he exemplifies!"

Philippe's exploits have inspired a similar kind of awe in me—and a similar pride in belonging to the human race.

The question I want to ask is why.

What he does is not, strictly speaking, art, is it? Nor does it fall within the domain of sports. From one point of view, I suppose it could be classified as an act of madness. After all, why risk your life for something that is at bottom utterly useless—a meaningless gesture? And yet, as I explain in the DVD interview, when I saw the footage of the Nôtre Dame walk, my eyes filled with tears when Philippe started juggling the wooden pins as he stood on the wire. It was so implausible, so terribly crazy, so beyond anything we can normally expect from a human being, that something inside me cracked.

For years, I have walked around with an idea for a documentary film (something I know I will never do) called *The Art of the Useless*. It would begin with a master cabinetmaker at work on the construction of an elaborate cupboard (utilitarian craft) interspersed with images of young girls in a ballet class straining to perfect their art (the quest for beauty, which is essentially useless, since it serves no practical purpose) and then move on to interviews and performances by various practitioners of neglected and under-appreciated "artistic" pursuits: Philippe and the high wire; Ricky Jay, the sleight-of-hand artist and "up-close" magician; and Art Spiegelman, the cartoonist who turned the comic book into serious literature—in other words, arts generally associated with children and carnivals, and yet in the case of these three men, pursued with such rigor, intelligence, and originality that these popular forms are lifted to great heights of sophistication. I have known each of them for many years, and they have many traits in common: monomania, ferocious discipline, a sense of historical perspective (each one is an obsessive collector of material concerning his art), and the ability to write well. (I would signal Ricky's history of magic, *Learned Pigs & Fireproof Women*, as an impressive example.)

The point being, I suppose, that by skirting past the traditional arts (literature, theater, music, painting), one could arrive at a better understanding of the aesthetic impulse in human beings, that the best argument for the importance of art lies precisely in its uselessness, that we are most deeply and powerfully human when we do things for the pure pleasure of doing them—even if it requires untold years of hard work and training (the young ballerinas) and even if the pleasure can entail frightening risk (the high wire). . . .

All that said, I hope you enjoy the film if you haven't already seen it.

Concerning your letter: I don't see any flaw at the heart of *Giving Offense*, which I consider to be an excellent book, and I doubt that the reason you are thick-skinned vis-à-vis your reviewers has anything to do with the fact that you earned your living as a teacher. You believe in your work, that's all there is to it. You believe in it and know that it's good.

Some months ago, we were wondering why no new sports had been invented in recent decades. Having taken a couple of peeks at the Winter Olympics, I think we might have overstated our case. Ski cross! Snowboarding! Women tumbling head over heels in midair with skis attached to their feet!

My heart was in my throat.

All best,

Paul

P.S.: On the heels of the German publication of *The Shaking Woman* last month, Siri has now been invited to give the annual lecture at the Freud Foundation in Vienna. Imagine. How not to be proud of her?

Paul Auster and J. M. Coetzee

Dear Paul,

Thanks very much for the Philippe Petit DVD, with the welcome bonus of a filmed interview with you. I enjoyed the interview. There is the pleasure of having you visit our living room, of hearing the enviably considered, just, and well-formed sentences you speak. Also the admirable generosity of your view of Petit himself, who strikes me, I am afraid to say, as a rather conceited fellow. But then, perhaps one needs to be conceited, or at least to have no doubts about oneself, if one is to prosper in funambulism or any other métier that requires absorption of the mental self in the physical self, an absorption that is indistinguishable—as you point out in the interview—from concentrated thought.

The film itself, I thought, was ill conceived. The moments that I bear away from it are still shots of Petit on the wire, taken from so far away that the wire vanishes and he seems to be standing in space. Too much of the rest of the movie consists of Petit promoting himself, telling us how "impossible" the feats are that he is about to perform, though we already know they were not impossible, since he performed them. All the tiresome recounting of how he and his friends evaded patrolling guards could also have been cut.

I can conceive of a better story about a funambulist than the one Petit embodies, a story that might have been sketched by Kafka in his early years and then discarded. A young man ventures out on a high wire over an abyss. He does not fall, he comes back safely, but he never ventures on the wire again, never even talks about it, though his friends remember his feat and reminisce about it among themselves. The young man resumes his life, eventually marries, has children, and in every outward respect prospers. Yet he is never his old self again: his friends know it, and so does he. It is as if he had met someone or something out in space, in the brief time he was there: a look passed, a recognition, and everything was changed.

What I want, I suppose, is not the actual Philippe Petit but a high-wire artist who is open to the metaphysical. But perhaps being open to the metaphysical is incompatible with having unquestioned faith that you are not going to fall.

Which brings me to a comment you made in your last letter to the effect that, as a writer, I seem to have solid faith in what I am doing. (You were responding to my remark that, hard though it might be to credit, I don't get upset when reviewers give me a going-over.)

I think that for once you are wrong about me. I don't have a great deal of faith in what I am doing. To be more precise, I have enough faith to get me through the writing itself— enough faith or perhaps enough hope, blind or blinkered hope, that if I give the project at hand enough time and attention it will "work," will not be a palpable failure. But that is where my faith or hope runs out. I don't have much faith that my work will endure. "Not marble, nor the gilded monuments / Of princes, shall outlive this powerful rhyme": that's what true faith sounds like. I can't echo it.

On quite another subject, I have been looking back at some remarks I made to you a while ago about the so-called global financial crisis, to the effect that it did not look to me like a real crisis, but on the contrary like a textbook example of people sitting in Plato's cave, staring at shadows (on their computer monitors), which they mistook for reality. I suggested that if we simply reset the numbers, the "crisis" would be over.

This prescription of mine, it might be objected, is much like saying that if we scooped out the contents of everyone's memories and replaced them with a new set of memories we would in effect be creating a new reality. What both prescriptions ignore, the objection might continue, is that memories are not just biochemical configurations in the brain (or configurations of bits in a computer) but the traces of things that really happened in a real past. Even the figures in the banks of monitors in the stock exchange have behind them a history from which they cannot be cut off—what we might call the historical memory of economics. In other words, the radical-idealist solution to the problem of how to make a better future (replace the past with a better past) is no more naive than the radical-idealist solution to the financial crisis: replace the bad figures with good ones.

To me (to skip several steps in the argument) the question boils down to how seriously we should take Jorge Luis Borges. Borges posits the irruption into our history (that is, into the body of historical memory that we broadly share) of an encyclopedia that, when completed, will have the potential to supplant the old past with a new past and thus a new present—that will, potentially, remake us. Is Borges's fable to be enjoyed as a philosophical *jeu d'esprit* but not taken seriously, or is he floating an idea with real philosophical depth? I would like to think the latter.

Applied to the financial crisis, the Borgesian proposal seems to me at least feasible, in theory. Compared with the weight and density of human history, the numbers on the computer monitors don't come trailing all that much historical freight behind them—not so much that we could not, if we truly wanted it, agree to dispense with them and start with a fresh set of numbers.

It is the question of whether we truly want a new financial dispensation, whether we can agree on a new set of figures, that is the rub. The figures themselves offer no resistance: the resistance is in ourselves. So, looking around us today, we see just what we might expect: we, "the world," would rather live through the misery of the reality we have created (the entirely artificial reality of the crisis) than put together a new, negotiated reality.

All the best,

John

Paul Auster and J. M. Coetzee

Dear John,

Just back from another brief journey . . . to find your new fax waiting for me.

So glad you enjoyed the filmed interview (which was done in cramped circumstances in no time at all), and yes, even if the words we have used are different—my "arrogant" as opposed to your "conceited"—there is no question that Philippe is a handful. I suppose that goes without saying. And yet, his very lack of humility is, I think, what makes him so interesting to me.

I understand your reservations about the film, but the images of that little man alone on the wire are unforgettable, and I was also much taken by the old footage from the early seventies of Philippe and his friends cavorting in the French countryside as he prepared for the big walk. A touching glimpse of the silliness and energy of youth—reminding me of outtakes from a Truffaut film that was never made. As for the interviews, the truth is that he is calmer and more charming in person. I sensed that he was very wound up while talking to the camera, determined to provide the director with a "good performance."

Forgive me if you feel I've misjudged you. I imagine my comments were a reflection of my own unbounded faith in your work. Of course you live with doubts and insecurities and a belief that your books will not endure. So do I. So, I would think, does every writer who is not certifiably insane. It is an inner condition, which has nothing to do with the good or bad things reviewers might say about us—since they always seem to praise for the wrong reasons, just as they condemn for the wrong reasons, which disqualifies them from serious consideration as arbiters of literary merit. Every writer judges himself—most often harshly—which is probably why writers keep writing: in the vain hope they will do better next time. But just because you (J.C.) live in doubt about yourself doesn't mean that I, as your reader of many years, need have any doubts about your work. As for one's response to reviews, it might simply be a matter of temperament—the thick-skinned versus the thin-skinned. Perhaps you are thick-skinned—at least when it comes to the remarks of strangers. I would not describe myself as thin-skinned—but thin-skinned enough to be happy with my decision not to read reviews anymore.

(News flash. I have just been on the phone with Paola Novarese of Einaudi and have two bits of information to pass on to you. First: it seems that both of us have been victims of a journalistic hoax. Over the past years, a certain Tommaso Debenedetti has been publishing fabricated interviews with writers in various newspapers—over twenty of them, apparently, perhaps even more—including one with you as far back as 2003 and one with me as recently as January of this year. A scandal in the works. I am not so much angry as confused. Why would someone go to so much trouble to fake encounters with writers—who, as we know, are the least important people in the world? Second: we will both be in Italy at the same time in June. Siri and I accepted to do a conversation together for a little Mondadori/Einaudi festival in Tuscany. One hour of discomfort for four days of vacation in the region afterward. According to Paola, you will be doing something in Genoa

Paul Auster and J. M. Coetzee

that same weekend [12–13]. It would be ludicrous not to make an effort to see each other during that time, even if it means spending an extra day or two in Italy before flying home. We would be more than willing to displace ourselves and strike out in your direction if a get-together is possible. Will Dorothy be with you? Let me know what you think. I'm sure that the people at Einaudi would be happy to help us with the arrangements.)

Mulling over your comments about the economic crisis, Borges, and new paradigms, I was most struck by your final remark that "we . . . would rather live through the misery of the reality we have created . . . than put together a new, negotiated reality." This applies not only to economics but to politics and nearly every social problem we are faced with. At random, let me set forth three examples from hundreds if not thousands of problems bedeviling the world.

1. The Mideast conflict. Whether or not one subscribes to Zionism, whether or not one believes in the logic of a secular state founded by the members of a single religion, Israel is a fact, and the destruction of Israel would cause irreparable harm to nearly everyone on the planet. World War III, untold numbers of deaths, incalculable disaster. On the other hand, in spite of the historical connection of the Jewish people to the region, Israel's Arab neighbors look upon the Jewish state as a cancer in their midst, and since 1948 they have been unrelenting in their determination to wipe it off the map. There was a time (before the assassination of Rabin, before the 9/11 attacks and the growth of militant Islam) when I felt some cautious optimism about the possibility of a two-state solution. Now that hope is gone, and when I consider that this conflict has

endured for what amounts to *my entire life*, I believe the time is long past due to begin thinking about radical and hitherto unimagined solutions. I have come up with several quixotic ideas over the years, but I believe my latest plan is the best. Evacuate the entire Israeli population and give them the state of Wyoming. Wyoming is immense and sparsely populated, and in the interests of world peace, the American government could simply buy up the ranches and farms there and relocate the Wyoming population to other states in the region. Why not? The greatest threat to mankind would be eliminated, Dick Cheney would be homeless, and in no time at all the Israelis would have established a thriving country. A perfectly rational solution, it seems to me, and yet of course it will never happen. Why? Because, to use your words, "we would rather live through the misery we have created."

2. The essential flaw of the United States Constitution. America purports to be a democracy (majority rule) but is in fact a country run by the few. I am not talking here about corporations, vested interests, and the economic elite, I am referring to the federal system itself, to the fact that each one of the fifty states has two senators, meaning that underpopulated Wyoming (approximately half a million people) has the same voice in the country's affairs as mega-populated California (more than thirty million people). Unfair and undemocratic, which means that we have a government that fails to express the will of its citizens. There are historical reasons for this flaw (the compromise of the 1780s that brought the original thirteen states together as a single country), but it was never a good idea, and now, more than two centuries later, it is threatening to tear us apart. How to change the system? Only through a

Paul Auster and J. M. Coetzee

congressional vote, which would ask the senators from the small states to vote themselves out of power, to eradicate themselves. And when has a politician ever voted himself out of power? And therefore we go on living in the misery we have created.

3. The crisis in American education. Everyone acknowledges the problem, everyone knows that the majority of our students are failing, everyone understands that an educated public is the only hope for the future of democracy (even if we are not, strictly speaking, a democracy), and yet every reform only seems to make the situation worse. My solution: better teachers. How to get better teachers? Pay them the same salaries as lawyers, doctors, and investment bankers, and suddenly the brightest students would begin opting for a career in teaching. It could easily be paid for by cutting X number of useless weapons projects, by reducing the military budget, but it will never happen, at least not in a world that resembles the one we live in today. And thus we go on wallowing in our misery.

I don't know how hard the economic crisis has hit Australia, but the effects have been devastating here. Not quite the out-and-out Great Depression we were girding ourselves against eighteen months ago, but horrible just the same, horrible for so many who have borne the brunt of it. Lost jobs, lost houses, the disintegration of whole towns and communities. As with every economic collapse in the past, every burst bubble since the beginning of capitalism, I think it was caused by historical blindness, an ignorant belief that what goes up need never come down, no matter how many times the up-down dynamic has played itself out in the past. In this case, the erroneous assumption that housing prices would go on rising forever. Therefore, sell houses to people who can't afford them, since in the end even they will come out on top. Then, even worse, bundle up those fragile, unsustainable mortgages into securities (a great word: *securities*), since everyone is bound to profit in a world that is all up and no down. Supposedly learned men subscribed to this nonsense, and now look at us. The scary part of it—at least here—is that no one in the world of finance seems chastened.

I have been reading Kleist lately, his stories and letters in particular. I remember being deeply impressed when I first read him in my early twenties, but now I am overwhelmed. His sentences are remarkable—great hatchet-blows of thought, an implacable narrative speed, a pulverizing sense of inevitability. No wonder Kafka liked him so much . . .

Tell me what your plans are for Italy in June. Siri and I would rejoice at seeing you again.

Best thoughts,

Paul

Dear Paul,

Thanks for your letter of April 7. I have been in contact with the folks at Einaudi, and I hope to see you and Siri in Pietrasanta in June.

Since you wrote, there have been further developments in the Debenedetti affair, as I am sure you must be aware. You and I turn out to be only two among a multitude of the man's victims. My Italian isn't up to much, but glancing at his made-up interview with me I infer that he uses me as a mouthpiece for certain views of his own about Africa and South Africa, in much the same way as he uses Philip Roth as a mouthpiece for his views on Barack Obama.

I haven't succeeded in locating the interview with you.

If this is his modus operandi, then his overall aim would seem to be to gather together a host of literary celebrities to spruik the Debenedetti vision of the world.

We live in an era in which it is really only the law of libel that holds back would-be writers like Debenedetti from turning us—and here *us* might include anyone whose name is more or less widely known—into characters in their fictions, making us mouth sentiments and perform actions that might amuse, upset, offend, repel, or even horrify us. If projects such as this flourish, then ultimately the pseudoselves that have been created for us, with their blessedly uncomplicated opinions, will come to reign in the public consciousness, while our "real" selves and our "true" (and tiresomely tangled) opinions will be known only to a few friends. The triumph of the simulacra.

You broach the subject of Israel. I find Israel hard to talk about, but if you will bear with me I will try to bring order to my tangled thoughts.

I follow the news from Israel/Palestine with feelings of such dismay and such distaste that sometimes it is a struggle not to simply pronounce a plague on both houses and turn away. A huge injustice has been done to the Palestinians—that we all recognize. They have been made to bear the consequences of events in Europe for which they were in no way responsible, and which—as you point out in your Wyoming-for-the-Jews fantasy—might have been resolved in half a dozen other ways that would not have involved chasing the Palestinians off their land.

But what is done is done, it can't be undone. Israel exists, and is going to exist for a long time. I know that Israeli politicians like to conjure up pictures of Arab armies swarming across the borders, slaughtering the men and raping the women and urinating on the ark of the temple, but the fact is that in half a century of trying their very best the Arabs haven't wrested back a square meter of Palestinian land; and there is no disinterested observer who believes that they would do any better if they tried a new invasion.

There is such a thing as defeat, and the Palestinians have been defeated. Bitter though such a fate may be, they must taste it, call it by its true name, swallow it. They must accept defeat, and accept it constructively. The alternative, unconstructive way is to go on nourishing revanchist dreams of a tomorrow when all wrongs, by some miracle, will be righted. For a constructive way of accepting defeat they might look to Germany post-1945.

What I call dreams of ultimate revenge Palestinians would

call dreams of ultimate justice. But defeat is not about justice, it is about force, greater force. As long as Israelis can see, simmering beneath the surface of Palestinian pleas for a just settlement, dreams of an ultimate turning of the tables, they will continue to be lukewarm—less than lukewarm—about a negotiated settlement.

What the Palestinians need is someone big enough to say, "We have lost, they have won, let us lay down our arms and negotiate the best terms of surrender we can, bearing it in mind, if it is any comfort, that the whole world will be watching." In other words, they need a great man, a man of vision and courage, to emerge from among themselves onto the stage. Unfortunately, when it comes to the vision-and-courage department, the leaders whom the Palestinians have produced thus far strike me as midgets. And if by some chance a savior were to emerge, my guess is that he would pretty soon be gunned down.

Perhaps the time has come for the women of Palestine to take over the reins.

Having said what I have said about the Palestinians, I must go on to say that there is something so ugly in the way that successive Israeli governments have behaved—democratically elected governments, working under a bad, bad constitution which will never be changed save by extra-constitutional action—that one's stomach is truly turned. There is only one word that will describe what has been done of late in Lebanon and Gaza, and that word is *schrecklich*. *Schrecklichkeit*: an ugly, hard word—a Hitlerian word—for an ugly, hard, heartless way of treating people. For any of us who might be inclined to entertain the essentially progressive notion that the history of humankind teaches lessons that we should heed if we want to become better people, the question that must give us pause is: What kind of lesson has history taught Israel?

I lived most of my life in South Africa, where there were plenty of whites who spoke about blacks along the same gamut, extending from amiable condescension to outright contempt to visceral hatred, that one hears employed when Israelis—many, many Israelis—speak about Arabs. There are "good" Israelis (I have met some of them; they are the salt of the earth), as there were "good" whites in the old South Africa. But there is no comforting lesson lurking here. If the "bad" South African whites were defeated, it was not because the "good" whites persuaded them of the wrongness of their ways and led them to repentance. If the "bad" Israelis are ever to be defeated, it will not be because the "good" Israelis will have shamed them. It will be for quite different reasons, which are as yet invisible to us.

Because I am seen as being on the Left, I am asked to sign petitions on behalf of the Palestinians and generally to support their cause. Sometimes I do as I am asked, sometimes I don't; always the decision demands soul-searching. In this respect I am sure I am not unique. Like many other Western intellectuals, including many non-Jewish Western intellectuals, I have divided feelings about Israel/Palestine.

There are two reasons why I in particular should feel divided. The first is that the Jewish element in Western culture has had a formative effect on me. I would not be who I am without Freud or Kafka, to say nothing of that aberrant Jewish prophet Jesus of Nazareth. Whereas Arab culture and Muslim religious thought, whatever their objective stature, have done nothing to shape me.

Of course Freud and Kafka mean nothing to Benjamin Netanyahu, who is the heir of the worst in the Jewish past, not the best. I have no qualms about hoping fervently for the downfall of Netanyahu and his cohort, and the arrival of a new leadership with the cojones to stand up to the Jewish Right.

But there is a second consideration. I have Jewish friends to whom the fate of the state of Israel means a great deal. If I have to choose between my friends and the principle of historical justice, I am afraid to say I choose my friends—not just because they are my friends but because I believe their commitment to Israel (which is not necessarily support for any particular Israeli government) is deeply thought out and deeply felt and at certain times quite anguished. I don't share in that commitment, but as in love, where the beloved is right even when she is wrong, so too in friendship.

As for Kleist, I agree with every word you say. To open a page by Kleist is to have it brought home to you that there exists an A league of writers, which has very few members and in which the game being played is very different from the game in the more comfortable B league to which one is accustomed: much harder, much quicker, much smarter, for much bigger stakes.

(By the way, I recently watched again Éric Rohmer's adaptation of Kleist's *Marquise von O.* I see the film as a tribute on the part of civilization—Rohmer had so civilized a sensibility that I am surprised he made any headway in the film world—to the mystery of genius.)

All the best,

John

Dear John,

So sorry that the fax machine was unplugged. We are in the midst of repairing the front steps of the house, and one of the workers apparently used the outlet for an electric tool and then forgot to put the fax plug back in place. Then, when your letter came through yesterday, I discovered that the ink cartridge had nearly given out. The first two pages are perfectly clear, but there are fuzzy areas on pages 3 and 4. I believe I have managed to decipher everything you wrote, but just to be sure, I wonder if you could resend those pages when you have the time.

Needless to say, Siri and I are both delighted that we will be crossing paths with you in June. If I'm not mistaken, it will be our fifth encounter in approximately two and a half years. Not bad when you consider the distance between Adelaide and New York. Also (and this must be a record of some kind), each encounter will have taken place in a different country. Australia, France, Portugal, America, and now Italy.

As for the Debenedetti business, no, I have not kept up with further developments. Is there a site on the Internet giving out new information? I would be curious to have a look. The fake interview with me was published in a newspaper called (I believe) *Il Nazionale*. Apparently, he submitted a second interview somewhere else, but the editor was suspicious and refused to run it. I glanced at the one that was published, and when I saw myself comparing New York City to a woman, I knew beyond a doubt that the piece was bogus. I have said many stupid things in my life, but nothing quite that stupid.

For reasons that have everything to do with why we have been writing to each other, everything to do with why we persist, I was heartened by your response to my comments about Kleist. Yes. And yes. And yes to all you have added.

It turns out that Siri and I are leaving for Jerusalem on April 30th and will be staying there for eight or nine days. So your comments about Israel have come at just the right moment. (I include an article from this morning's *New York Times*, read over breakfast an hour ago. Not a terribly profound piece, but it does seem to capture something about what's going on over there—along with the depressing but unfortunately accurate words: "the shrinking political left.")

You mention "tangled thoughts." Given how tangled the situation is, how tangled it has always been, I don't see how any other kinds of thoughts are possible. My joke solution to repatriate the Israelis to Wyoming is yet another example of tangled thinking—and also an expression of absolute despair, a conviction that the two sides will never be able to come to terms. As Amos Oz has said, "Make peace, not love." But not even that seems likely anymore.

Tangled, and also, as you say, *divided*. Even I, a Jew born one year before the founding of the state of Israel, am no less divided than you are.

We all know why Israel was created, we can all readily imagine (or remember) the climate immediately after World War II and understand why so many believed a Jewish state was necessary. But that doesn't mean it was ever a good idea. Sadly, there is no going back, and, as you say, what is done is done and cannot be undone.

There is no doubt that both sides have behaved badly. Israeli expansion into the West Bank after the 1967 war has created an intolerable situation, which only seems to become more intolerable as the years pass. The suffering and degradation of the Palestinians is an outrage. And as the right wing grows ever stronger in Israel, the galling thing to me is that many of the settlers are *Americans*—for the most part young, fanatically religious Orthodox Jews from Brooklyn who have moved over there to live out the cowboy-and-Indian fantasies of their childhoods. They are crazy people, beyond the pull of reason, and their very presence stands in complete contradiction to the kind of country Israel was supposed to be when it was founded: secular, socialist, tolerant.

For years, I have been saying more or less the same thing you expressed in your letter about the Palestinian leadership. If, instead of Arafat, there had been a Middle Eastern Gandhi to frame the political discourse, I am convinced the Palestinians would have had a country of their own twenty or thirty years ago. Then, too, there is the repulsive hypocrisy of the surrounding Arab countries, countries so rich from their oil revenues that they easily could have sent vast amounts of money to the Palestinians to help build a viable, prosperous society there. But they stand by and do nothing, preferring to let the Palestinians suffer as a propaganda tool against Israel.

Because of my tangled thoughts, my tangled feelings, I resisted going to Israel until I was almost fifty. Then an invitation came from the Jerusalem Foundation (run by Teddy Kollek) to spend three or four weeks as "writer in residence" at the Mishkenot Sha'ananim, and I decided to accept. So off I went with Siri and the nine-year-old Sophie in January of 1997.

The awful Netanyahu was prime minister, and because I gave an interview in which I called him "stupid and evil," I was attacked rather harshly by the right-wing press, particularly the *Jerusalem Post*. But no matter. I still stand by what I said, and the truth is that during our visit we only met the sort of people you would call "good Israelis"—and yes, we found them to be the salt of the earth, extraordinarily vibrant, thoughtful, sympathetic souls.

Nevertheless, the impression I came away with was that the greatest threat to Israel was not the Palestinians but the Israelis themselves, that the country was so split (roughly fourteen months after the assassination of Rabin) that there was a possibility of civil war. Now, I am told, a general feeling of apathy has settled over the population, nearly everyone is tired of politics, and the young people are altogether unengaged. In a little more than a week, I will have a chance to judge for myself.

More to follow . . .

With warmest thoughts,

Paul

Dear John,

We have returned from the Land of Torment. All the fears I had about going back to Israel after thirteen years have been borne out by what I saw and heard and felt there. Bad as the situation was in 1997, it is far worse now. The "good Israelis" (as you called them in your last letter) are living in a state of despair. The others are locked in a ferocious and obdurate denial.

The tragedy is all the more terrible because it is taking place in one of the most beautiful cities on earth. Jerusalem in flower, the May light, the gravity of the stones, resplendent colors everywhere. And yet, underneath it all, madness and hatred, the death of hope. As a friend who lives in Tel Aviv put it: "Jerusalem is no longer a city. It is an epidemic, a disease."

Nevertheless, on the surface, life continues. The literary festival was well organized, writers attended from all over the world, the events drew large crowds. Intellectuals and artists seem to be thriving, and both Siri and I were impressed by many of the people we met. But no one—barring a few exceptions—has any interest in talking about the "Situation" anymore. Most seem worn out, sick to death of the whole business.

There were, inevitably, a few encounters with journalists. The first question they all asked was: "Did you have any doubts or second thoughts about coming to Israel?" And then, at some point, one would be asked to comment on the "Situation"—the same subject few Israelis have the heart to discuss anymore. It is the only country I know of where such a question is possible. A foreign writer visiting France or Italy would not be asked to comment on French or Italian politics. At most, one would be asked to comment on conditions in one's own country. But the Israeli journalists I met had no interest in hearing me talk about America—only America as it relates to Israel. Again and again, I had to insist that Obama is not anti-Israel, that the demands he is making on the Israelis to stop building new settlements are the only way to prevent the country from pursuing its suicidal national policy.

All countries have their problems, of course. But no other country feels that its very existence is threatened, that annihilation is a distinct possibility. Fear blinds the Israelis, which makes them forget that they are the only military superpower in the region. Fear makes them self-obsessed, walled off from the rest of the world.

Putting aside the larger question of Palestine, the two-state solution, and the deadlock that has continued for the past forty-three years, what distressed me most was the attitude of Jewish Israelis toward Arab Israelis—who now comprise, I think, 18% of the population. When you consider that the United States is only 12% black and that those 12% play a significant role in the life of the country, it is shocking to see how little interaction there is between the majority and the minority in Israel. The Arabs are *citizens*, and yet their fellow citizens want nothing to do with them. At best, the Jews support the old idea of "separate but equal"—which, to my American ears, sounds grotesquely familiar. I would not go so far as to call Israel an apartheid state, but it is very close to a Jim Crow society, which is depressing enough.

Worst of all: the fences, the so-called security barriers. My heart sank the first time I saw one, and then I said to myself: this is a country invented by Jonathan Swift.

The principal reason for going there was to spend some time with our friend David Grossman. He and his wife are still mourning their son (who was killed nearly four years ago), but the meals and conversations we had with them somehow made the visit worthwhile, in spite of everything. By some lucky twist, it turns out that David will be going to the Mondadori/ Einaudi weekend in Italy next month. Impossible to tell you how much I am looking forward to seeing you there, to spending a few days with you again.

With best thoughts,

Paul

Dear Paul,

Thanks for your letter of May 11, reporting on your visit to what you call the Land of Torment. I don't sympathize much with today's Israelis, or at least with those who voted Netanyahu into office, but having lived through the 1970s and 1980s in South Africa, I find the mixture of paranoia, belligerence, and pessimism that you describe all too familiar.

There has been, of late, a fair amount of work by South African historians exploring the way in which the South African government moved or found itself moved from Israeli-type intransigence to a more or less bloodless surrender of power. It would appear that there were intelligent people in the government and the armed forces who as early as 1980 realized that whites could not forever maintain their monopoly of power. What kept them from speaking out was a well-founded fear of being cast into a political or professional wilderness.

Thus a paradoxical situation developed in which the ruling elite came to include a growing number of people who knew that apartheid was a dead end but allowed themselves to be trapped in silence, while the actual exercise of power gravitated more and more into the hands of the last true believers, the extremists of the Right.

If something analogous is going on behind the scenes in Israel right now, then perhaps there may be hope after all. One scenario: power passes from the Netanyahu types to the Lieberman types, then in reaction there is some kind of extra-constitutional palace revolution.

Getting the army generals onside was the great achievement of F. W. de Klerk. It was something he did behind the scenes before he made his dramatic reforming moves. Maybe in Israel, some day, the army will force the politicians to come to their senses. Wishful thinking? You know the country better than I do.

Seeing you and Siri in Pietrasanta, even if it was only briefly, was the high point of this late trip. The Einaudi people were most kind to bring us together.

I've been to enough cultural events in Italy by now not to be unnerved by the chaos that seems to envelop them. No one is sure exactly where the session is to take place, the man who looks after the sound system cannot be located, the interpreter is up in arms because no one has informed her of the running order, etcetera, etcetera. Yet when the hour arrives, everything goes off smoothly: the audience miraculously knows where to come, the sound system works, the interpreter does a first-class job. The chaos turns out to have been spurious: we can run an event perfectly efficiently, the Italians seem to be saying, without fetishizing efficiency—in fact, we can turn the running of an event into a diverting little comic drama of its own.

After saying good-bye to you in Pietrasanta I went on to Genoa. After Genoa I was planning to take a leisurely train ride to Toulouse. But the hand of God intervened in the shape of floods and washaways in the Tarn valley. The trains stopped running, and I had to find a flight out of Nice.

Back in Adelaide, I am eight hours out of phase with life around me, and in the present cold and overcast weather find it hard to readjust my body clock. So I am staying up all night and sleeping in the day. One incidental boon is that I can watch the World Cup football live.

I have never been a true aficionado of The Beautiful Game, and what I see from South Africa does little to change my mind. There can't be another sport in which players spend so much of their time fouling one another and generally infringing the rules behind the referee's back. The fact that the all-seeing eye of the television camera captures their petty cheating and transmits it worldwide seems to make no difference to them. A reign of shamelessness.

All the best,

John

Dear John,

Many thanks for your letter, which I have just found in the fax machine downstairs. I was going to ask Siri to send you another e-mail with a two-word message—"Fax fixed"—but clearly you have figured this out for yourself.

Yes, it was an enormous pleasure seeing you in Italy. The trip to Lucca, the good food, the talk. Too little time, of course, but something is undoubtedly better than nothing. We will have to have another rendezvous in the not too distant future, although I'm afraid it won't happen until you go to Toronto in the fall of 2011. Perhaps you (and Dorothy?) can visit us in New York afterward—or, if that isn't possible, perhaps Siri and I can meet you in Canada, which isn't far from here, at least not when compared to going to Australia.

Like you, I started following the World Cup because of jet lag. In America, the games are aired early in the morning and early in the afternoon, and because I have been getting up *very* early since returning from Europe, I quickly fell into the habit of switching on the TV to watch. Sports fiend that I am, I have become more and more engrossed. You probably played football (soccer) as a boy. I didn't, and therefore my knowledge of the game is far more superficial than yours. I agree with you that the fouling and feigning are stupid and embarrassing, altogether at odds with the stoical, "good sportsman" attitude I grew up with, but if The Beautiful Game is not always beautiful, it does provide its pleasures. The grit of a so-so American team coming back from deficits again and again, the composure of the Dutch in defeating the Brazilians, the speed and precision of the Germans. I am pulling for Holland, the brilliant also-rans of cups past, but I'm afraid the Germans will be too strong for them. (By the time this letter reaches you, we'll know if my prediction was accurate or not.)

What befuddles me about the sport, however, is the role of the clock. The game plunges on without any stoppage, players dawdle, delay, roll around on the pitch in two-minute-long group hugs after each goal is scored, and then, at the end of each half, the referee arbitrarily tacks on some additional time. In the clock sports I am most familiar with—basketball and American football—"clock management" is an essential part of the game. Every time the ball goes out of bounds, the clock stops. A basketball team must shoot within twenty-four seconds; a football team must execute its next offensive play within forty-five. All this makes sense to me. In soccer, however, there is a kind of lethargy or laxness that seems to undermine the importance of the clock—which is a contradiction, since it is a game ruled by the clock. Am I making sense?

I doubt that I know or understand Israel any better than you do, having been there only twice. The comparison you make with the end of apartheid in South Africa is tantalizing, seductive, perversely hopeful, but . . . I'm not sure. The situation in South Africa was essentially an internal one: a racist government oppressing the majority of its citizens. But South Africa wasn't threatened by anyone outside its borders, which is sadly the case in Israel. Much as I despise the Israeli government for its hardheaded positions, lapses in judgment, and frequent acts of cruelty, there is no question that the threat is real. The one positive step the Israelis have taken in the last years—evacuating Jewish settlements in Gaza—has led to multiple catastrophes. The election of Hamas, thousands of rockets launched across the border, the blockade—to name just a few. You wonder if the Israeli army might one day turn against the government. Possibly yes, but it strikes me as the longest of long shots. Simply because the government can keep the military in line by pointing to the constant threats—real or imagined—from Israel's neighbors.

I sometimes think that the best way to unblock the standoff would be a *one*-state solution. Abandon the principles of Zionism, declare the West Bank and Gaza part of Israel, and give all Arabs equal rights as citizens. But then I tell myself that this plan could never work. Israel would turn into Belgium. A bloody, hate-infested Belgium.

A few days before we left for Europe in early June, an article was published in the *New York Times Book Review* by American novelist Jonathan Franzen about the seventieth anniversary of the publication of Christina Stead's *The Man Who Loved Children*. Not a bad article, really; on the whole quite astute and generous, but the piece began with the following paragraph, which I found deeply strange:

> There are any number of reasons you shouldn't read *The Man Who Loved Children* this summer. It's a novel, for one thing; and haven't we all secretly sort of come to an agreement, in the last year or two or three, that novels belonged to the age of newspapers and are going the way of newspapers, only faster? As an old English professor friend of mine likes to say, novels are a curious moral

case, in that we feel guilty about not reading more of them but also guilty about doing something as frivolous as reading them; and wouldn't we all be better off with one less thing in the world to feel guilty about?

Franzen has had enormous success here—both critically and commercially. He is a man who has spent his life writing novels, which would suggest, I presume, that he believes in the practice of reading novels. Why then would he launch this attack against . . . himself? The article, after all, was written for a weekly magazine devoted exclusively to books, which means that any person who bothered to read the article necessarily has an interest in books, is necessarily a reader of books, not only of nonfiction but of novels—the very thing Franzen is telling him he should no longer be interested in. I scratch my head in bafflement.

Siri's eighty-seven-year-old mother is with us now, and we will be taking her to Norway the day after tomorrow for a family reunion. I dread the thought of going on yet another plane, but we have to do this. It could well be Siri's mother's last trip home, and duty calls. We return on the fifteenth, at which point I plan to lock myself in a room and keep my feet on the ground for the rest of the summer.

> With sweaty greetings on this
> ninety-eight-degree day,

Paul

Dear Paul,

In the wake of the recent World Cup (football), I have been ruminating on the question of why it is that you and I, you no longer as young as you once were and I positively aged, spend so much time watching sports that we can no longer play.

The answer is, I suppose, that both us see in organized sport, and the spectacle of sport devoured by so many people, one of the major social phenomena of our age. We see that and maybe also approve of it—approve of sport in and of itself and the vicarious participation in sport too.

So we think sport is a good thing. But why? For manly sports certainly do not turn one into a better person—there are too many instances of people who excel at sports but are no great shakes as human beings. Yet perhaps there is a certain elephant in the room that we ignore. Bearing in mind what I wrote a while ago about it perhaps being a good thing if the Palestinians would learn to swallow defeat, I'd like to relay some thoughts I have been having about losing in sport.

Think of professional tennis. Thirty-two men take part in a tournament. Half of them will lose in the first round and go home without having tasted any of the sweetness of victory. Of the sixteen who remain another eight will go home having tasted a single victory and then defeat and expulsion. Humanly speaking, the predominating experience of the tournament will be of defeat.

Or take boxing. A boxer makes it to Caesar's Palace with a record of thirty-two wins and three losses behind him. But what of the thirty-two guys he defeated, who will never make it to Caesar's Palace or any other glamorous venue? What of the guys who never win a single fight, the professional losers, men who are shoved into the ring only because there can't be a winner unless there is also a loser?

In sports there are winners and there are losers; what no one bothers to say (is it too obvious?) is that there are many more losers than there are winners. In the Tour de France, which is being contested as I write, there were something like 200 starters, of whom one will come out the winner on overall time while 199 will be nonwinners, i.e., no matter what consoling stories they may tell themselves, losers.

Sport teaches us more about losing than about winning, simply because so many of us don't win. What it teaches above all is that it is OK to lose. Losing is not the worst thing in the world, because in sports, unlike in war, the loser doesn't get to have his throat cut by the winner.

Think of that profoundly interesting moment in a small boy's life when he graduates from pretend sport, in which the adults or the older boys allow him to win all the time and generally to feel he is a little king, to the real thing, where if you don't hit the ball you are out, you have to give up the bat to someone better than you and retire ingloriously. It comes as a shock to the little boy's psychic system. He wants to bawl, throw a tantrum, try all the tricks that work with his parents. He wants to subject reality to his ego. But it gets him nowhere. "Stop sniffling, kid!" But also: "Stop sniffling, kid—you'll get another turn."

Because that is the great lesson of sport. You lose most of the time, but *as long as you stay in the game* there will always be a tomorrow, a fresh chance to redeem yourself.

In this great school of losing, you don't flunk out unless you refuse to accept that you have lost, unless you reject the verdict of the game and retire into majestic isolation.

I would like to see the Israelis and the Palestinians playing football against each other once a month, with neutral referees. Then the Palestinians can learn that they can lose without losing everything (there is always next month's game), while the Israelis can learn that you can lose against Palestinians, and so what?

Thanks for the letter (July 5). A quick note on South African history ("South Africa wasn't threatened by anyone outside its borders"). In the 1980s the South African army and air force fought a major campaign against Cuban forces in Angola, and lost, or at least had to take losses they could not sustain. It was not just a matter of being outnumbered: the Cubans were flying Russian fighters that outmaneuvered and outgunned the South Africans' French Mirages. The generals went home and confronted the politicians. "The tide has turned against us," they said. "You have got to do something about it."

There are thousands (tens of thousands?) of Cubans buried in African soil. In Cuban eyes, their fraternal expedition to Angola counts as one of the high points in their history.

In your letter you quote the opening paragraph of a recent review by Jonathan Franzen, who in turn quotes a professor friend of his. I fear that the attitude expressed by the friend (a professor of English yet!) is all too typical. Professors of literature don't, by and large, keep up with what is being published in poetry and fiction, don't see it as part of their remit. If you want to meet people who read new fiction, you have to go to the book clubs and reading circles, where the readers are mainly women putting their liberal-arts degrees to some use. But I don't have to tell you this.

As for Franzen's own position—which from the extract you quote seems to me layered in irony—I suspect I am more sympathetic to him than you are. Faced with a choice between reading a run-of-the-mill novel and raking leaves in the garden, I think I would go for raking leaves. I don't get much pleasure out of consuming novels; and—more important—I think that indifference to reading fiction as a recreation is spreading in society. It has become quite respectable, at least among men, to say that one doesn't read fiction at all. I am a professional, with a professional stake in the business, so I can't use myself as a yardstick. But I must say that I get impatient with fiction that doesn't try something that hasn't been tried before, preferably with the medium itself.

All the best,

John

Dear John,

One of the reasons why I remain so attached to baseball after all these years is the very thing you write about in your letter: the frequency of losing, the inevitability of failure. A look at the standings in this morning's paper shows that the team with the best record this season has fifty-eight wins and thirty-four losses—which computes to a 63% success rate, meaning that the strongest team out of thirty has gone home frustrated 37% of the time.

Baseball seasons are very long—162 games—and each team goes through its ups and downs over the course of that six-month stretch: slumps and streaks, injuries, painful losses that turn on a single crucial play, unexpected last-second victories. Unlike boxing—which is always do or die—baseball is do *and* die, and even when you do die, you must crawl out of your coffin the next day and give it your best shot again. It is for this reason that steadiness of temper is so highly valued in baseball. Shrug off defeats, take victories in stride, without undue exaltation. The common wisdom is that baseball mirrors life—in that it teaches you how to take the good with the bad. Most other sports tend to mirror war.

There have been many strange doings in the athletic universe this summer. The longest set in tennis history, bizarre errors by referees in the World Cup, the official return to the female sex by the South African runner whose name escapes me now. Most compelling of all, there was an incident that occurred a couple of months ago in a major league baseball game—not so much a story about sports as about human grace. By my rough calculations, approximately a quarter of a million baseball games have been played in the past 120 years. In all that time, only twenty perfect games have been thrown by pitchers—that is, games in which the pitcher has retired every batter on the other team from the beginning of the game to the end, twenty-seven batters in a row, three per inning for the full nine innings. A young pitcher from Detroit named Galarraga (very young, early twenties, just starting out, someone I had never heard of) was on the brink of entering the palace of immortality. He had retired the first twenty-six batters, and when the twenty-seventh was thrown out at first base, it appeared that the doors of the palace had opened and he had stepped across the threshold. The batter was clearly out (every replay from every angle proved this beyond a shadow of a doubt), but the first-base umpire, a man named Jim Joyce (James Joyce!) missed the call and said the batter was safe. This was a stupendous error, perhaps the worst officiating blunder in the history of the sport, and the beautiful thing about what happened at that moment, the moment when Galarraga understood that his perfect game had been unfairly stolen from him, was that the young man smiled. Not a smile of derision or contempt. Not even an ironical smile, but a genuine smile, a smile of wisdom and acceptance—as if he were saying, "Of course. Such is life, and what else can you expect?" I have never seen anything like it. Any other player in that situation would have erupted in a tantrum of anger and protest, screaming at the injustice of it all. But not this boy. Calmly, showing no hint of upset (for the game had to continue), he retired the twenty-eighth batter—

thereby completing a perfect game more perfect than any that had come before it, and one for which he will get no credit.

Afterward, when Jim Joyce saw the replay, he was mortified. "I robbed that kid of his perfect game," he said, and he publicly apologized to Galarraga—who graciously accepted the apology, saying that everyone makes mistakes and that he bore no grudge.

•

Forgive me for forgetting Angola. Stupid, stupid. But still, would you agree with me in saying that apartheid was an internal South African policy, and until international sanctions started quite late in the game, the world mostly stood around and watched for decades?

I don't know if you remember this, but it still burns in my mind, still fills me with anger: sometime in the seventies or eighties, the U.S. Congress made a symbolic declaration to the South African government, asking them to release Nelson Mandela from prison. The vote was nearly unanimous. Among the two or three dissenters: Dick Cheney.

•

As for the reading of novels, I think novelists themselves should be exempted from the discussion. You can't read other people's novels while you are writing your own. And when we do read them, needless to say we don't want to read mediocre ones. Raking leaves is surely preferable (and I detest raking leaves), but we mustn't forget the thrill we feel when we come across something truly good. And then—ah, and *then*—how to forget

Paul Auster and J. M. Coetzee

the passion of our reading when we were young, when it seemed that our very lives depended on it?

I realize that Franzen was trying to be funny—or ironic—or provocative in his opening paragraph. It's simply that the joke fell flat for me. The contempt in America for anything related to artistic or intellectual pursuits is so widespread today, so deeply a part of right-wing, populist thinking, that it pained me to see F. rehashing those ugly platitudes—even in jest. This is the country, after all, where George W. Bush, the scion of wealth and privilege, can pretend to be a "regular guy"—and get away with it—whereas Obama, who grew up in difficult circumstances, is seen as an "elitist" because he has written a couple of books, did well at Columbia and Harvard, and used to be a law professor.

•

We are back from Norway now, which I would have to describe as the Land of No Torment. Landscapes of unearthly beauty—literally, not of this earth, as if we had landed on some other planet. Siri's mother, who just six weeks ago appeared to be at death's door, has made a complete recovery after a doctor's misdiagnosis, and she was the queen of the family reunion (which included forty-nine people of all ages), the last living member of her generation, and therefore the matriarch, albeit a quiet, self-effacing one, basking in the affection of her children, her nieces and nephews, and the children of her children, nieces, and nephews. A wondrous thing to behold.

•

According to a note I received from Philip Roth the other day: "You should know that in the Italian press Debenedetti said that he plans to publish a book of his fabricated interviews with an introduction by me."

Apparently, the story goes on.

With best thoughts,

Paul

Dear Paul,

This morning I finished reading Philip Roth's *Exit Ghost*, and this evening I watched François Ozon's film *Le temps qui reste*. A common motif: cancer. *Exit Ghost* stars a septuagenarian who, impotent after prostatectomy, falls head over heels in love with a young woman. The film is about a rather vain and selfish young man who finds that he has terminal cancer and in the course of his last days becomes what one can only call a better human being. So: the one a comedy of cancer, of the bitter Rothian variety, the other an elegy of a quite affecting kind.

I don't find *Exit Ghost* a particularly notable addition to the Roth canon. I know that Roth relishes the challenge of wringing something fresh out of stock situations, but there is only so much mileage one can get out of the aging male struggling against decay to prove his virility one last time.

Otherwise with the Ozon film. Do you know his work? The film is perfect in its way, capturing the loneliness of the dying and the mix of compassion, indifference, and anxiety with which the rest of us treat them. It makes delicate use of a little inset story that in other hands might have come out grotesque: a waitress approaches the young man in a café, compliments him on his looks, and invites him to inseminate her, since her husband—who is complicit in the proposal—is sterile. She even offers to pay. The young man is at first offended, but in the end thinks better of it: it is a way of leaving something of himself behind.

There is a Chekhovian feel to this inset story as Ozon handles it: sympathetic yet cool and clear-eyed. The couple's rather anxious question to the young man, as they are saying goodbye: Can you reassure us that it is cancer you are suffering from (dying of) and not AIDS? He would clearly like to see them again; they have no such wish.

I assume you have read *Exit Ghost*, so you know that it is a bit of a ragbag. It includes an entirely unmotivated diatribe on trends in so-called cultural journalism put in the mouth of Roth's character Lonoff. In this diatribe there is no doubt much that I, as non–New Yorker, miss. But Lonoff (Roth too?) clearly feels nothing but contempt for the mixture of moralizing and biographical reductionism that passes for criticism in your cultural organs (ours too). (By biographical reductionism I mean treating fiction as a form of self-disguise practiced by writers: the task of the critic is to strip away the disguise and reveal the "truth" behind it.) The villain in *Exit Ghost* is one of these critics. He threatens to publish a reading of Lonoff's fiction as a disguised history (or perhaps an occluded history—one doesn't know) of incest with an elder sister.

I have no trouble understanding why Roth, a very visible figure on the literary landscape, should have strong feelings about this brand of literary criticism, even while he is aware that the more he fulminates, the more the Klimans of the world (Kliman is the critic-villain) lick their lips (*What is he trying to hide?*). I am sure that you, who swim in the same pond as Roth and are only slightly less visible, must have views of your own on the subject, which I think I can guess at. As for me, I like to think that, living on the very fringes of the known universe, I will escape the attention of the Klimans; but I am probably deluded.

Warmest wishes,

John

P.S.: I have no wish to extend the discussion of South African history unnecessarily, but if there had been no cold war the whole South African mess would have been settled much earlier. For decades the South African regime represented itself as a bastion against Russian penetration into minerals-rich sub-Saharan Africa, and one U.S. administration after another bought that story. It didn't help that the African National Congress was enmeshed with the South African Communist Party.

The old South African regime was only one of a rats' nest of dictatorships and oligarchies worldwide that the U.S. supported during the cold war for strategic ends. It was no coincidence that F. W. de Klerk unbanned the ANC in the same year that the Soviet Union was dissolved and the Berlin Wall fell.

Dear John,

Alas, I have not read *Exit Ghost*, nor have I seen *Le temps qui reste*. I have consumed several Roth novels over the years (no more than a fraction of his output) and have seen two or three Ozon films—one of which, *Swimming Pool*, made a strong impression on me.

Do I swim in the same pond as Roth? I'm not sure. We have crossed paths a few times, have twice had threesome dinners with Don DeLillo (a close friend of mine for many years), and have exchanged a handful of letters. In other words, he is an acquaintance, not a comrade. The thing that most interests him about me, I think, is the fact that we were both born in Newark. As for New York, however, I am not "slightly less visible" than he is—I am vastly less visible, perhaps infinitely less visible. Roth is a god whose work has been universally praised since his first book, whereas I am a mere struggling mortal whose work has been kicked around far more than I wish to remember. On top of that, I tend to steer clear of crowds, parties, and public pronouncements, preferring to tend my own little garden in Brooklyn. Roth, on the other hand, has been an enormous literary presence for more than fifty years—an exceptionally long run for any writer, no doubt the longest run of any American in history. One proof of his fame: he is the only living novelist whose work has been published by the Library of America.

Not having read *Exit Ghost*, I can't comment specifically on Lonoff's rant against contemporary cultural journalism, but from your description of it, I would say that it is spot-on.

Americans seem to have lost contact with the essence of fiction—which is to say, have lost the ability to understand the imagination—and therefore they find it difficult to believe that a novelist can "make things up." Every novel is turned into a hidden autobiography, a roman à clef. No need to elaborate on how impoverished this view is—nor how ugly it can become in the hands of a malicious journalist.

Your fax arrived last night while I was in the midst of watching my hapless baseball team (the New York Mets) suffer through yet another painful, extra-innings loss, and since we have written so much about sports lately, and since your letter discusses both a book and a film, I was fascinated to find the enclosed two articles in this morning's *New York Times*.

To begin with "E-Books Fly Beyond Mere Text." Everyone has an opinion about e-books, of course. It is the burning topic in publishing today, and there is no doubt that we are witnessing a revolution, one that seems to be gaining strength with each passing minute. Even though I fall into the category of technophobe, I feel no threat from or hostility to Kindles, Nooks, or iPads. Anything that encourages reading should be considered a good thing, and these devices are unquestionably a great boon to the literary traveler. Rather than lug around a suitcase with thirty books in it, you can now load those thirty books into a lightweight digital contraption and move from place to place unencumbered.

On the other hand, I do have certain fears. (Fears, by the way, already borne out by the destruction of the music business. How I miss browsing in record shops!) Amazon, which has so far cornered the market here, is selling books at too low a price, is in fact taking a loss with each book it sells in order to woo the public into buying the machines. One can foresee dire consequences in the long term: the collapse of publishing houses, the death of bookstores, a future in which every writer is his own publisher. As Jason Epstein pointed out in an article in the *New York Review* some months ago, it is absolutely essential that we continue to publish traditional paper books, that our libraries be maintained, since they are the bedrock of civilization. If everything went digital, think of the possible mischief that could ensue. Erased texts, vanished texts, or, just as frightening, altered texts.

Okay. Such is my opinion. What concerns me now is the article in this morning's paper and why I am of two minds about what I have read. The split seems to fall neatly between the terms "fiction" and "nonfiction." For months now, I have been doing research for the novel I have finally just begun, part of which will concern itself with America in the early fifties. Consequently, I have read book after book about the Korean War, the Red Scare, the polio epidemic, the H-bomb, and so forth, but have also been watching documentary films, which can be very helpful. When, in today's article, I came across the description of the "enhanced" *Nixonland*, I was intrigued. What an excellent idea, I thought, to combine written text and film in a history book. Such an excellent idea, in fact, that I can find no fault with it.

With the novels, however, I found myself resisting. The books mentioned are mass-market pop thrillers, but they are works of fiction for all that, and the notion of adding clips from a television series based on one of those books irks me. The question is why. Does it have something to do with the loss of belief in the imagination that I mentioned earlier? As if books

Paul Auster and J. M. Coetzee

are somehow too hard to absorb, and the story cannot be fully experienced until it is seen by the naked eye? But isn't reading the art of seeing things for yourself, of conjuring up images in your own head? And isn't the beauty of reading all about the *silence* that surrounds you as you plunge into the story, the sound of the author's voice resonating inside you to the exclusion of all other sounds?

Perhaps I have turned into a stodgy old man. There are critical editions of classic novels that include excised passages, alternative endings, and even photographs. Why not film as well? I don't know, but something in me is repelled by the notion of reading *Disgrace*, for example, and being able to click onto the film adaptation in midsentence on the second page of chapter 4. I am curious to know if you share this reaction or not.

Concerning "How Do You Pack a Stadium?" I feel equally confused. There is no question that one can now "see" a game better on television than in the stadium where the game is played. But, as the sixty-three-year-old fan says about going in person, "I just want the ambience, to watch the players and feel the crowd. I would much rather have the feel of the game brought into the home, not the other way around." The thirty-two-year-old fan disagrees (not without justification), but I'm not sure that turning an actual experience into a video experience is the answer. Especially at such a cost. How not to be stunned by an expenditure of $100 million on "stadium technology," not to speak of "personal seat licenses" going for as high as $20,000—just for the right to buy a ticket? It's not that I'm nostalgic for the old days, but I distinctly remember going to Yankee Stadium with a couple of my friends in 1961 (we were fourteen) to see the Giants versus the Browns and paying fifty cents for a seat in the bleachers. As we have been saying all along, sport is big business now, a mega-industry, a leviathan, and most of the world seems more than happy to be swallowed by the whale.

As for South Africa and its role in the cold war, you are of course 100% right. Not that you need to hear that from me.

New York continues to broil—the hottest July on record. When I wrote to you the other week and announced that the temperature was 98, I was wrong. It was 106.

With fondest good thoughts,

Paul

Dear Paul,

I recently received an alumnus magazine from a university in South Africa. It included an article celebrating the opening of the new university library, with computer stations and study cubicles and seminar rooms and work spaces too many to count. I read the article, reread it to make sure. I was right. The word *book* did not occur once.

In designing the library the architects had no doubt called on the advice of librarians, librarians of the new generation who look down on books as old-fashioned, whose dream is of a paperless library.

What do such people have against books? Why don't they share my vision of the library as acre upon acre of dimly lit stacks holding row upon row of tightly packed books stretching to infinity in every direction?

The argument against the Borgesian library is almost too tedious to rehearse—too tedious and too clinching, in an age in which economics has been elevated to queen of the sciences. It is that books take up too much space. There is no way of justifying the preservation of a physical object that occupies 20 cm by 15 cm by 3 cm of costly space, and may sit on a shelf for decades and centuries untouched, unread. If we drop our deceased loved ones into holes in the earth, or consign them to the flames, why should it be sacrilege to get rid of dead books?

Get rid of books, replace them with images of books, electronic images. Get rid of the dead, replace them with photographs.

I am dismayed at the prospect of the library of the future. I am sure that feeling is shared by many. But, aside from sentiment, what can justify such dismay? A hunger for the real in a world of shadows? Books are not real, not in any important sense. The very letters on the page are signs, images of sounds, which are images of ideas. The fact that what we call a book can be picked up in one's hands, has a smell and a feel of its own, is an accident of its production with no relevance to what the book conveys.

When I was sixteen, having some money to spend, I bought ten or so books that were going to constitute the foundation of a personal library. They included *War and Peace* in the translation by Aylmer Maude, published by Oxford University Press, a bulky little book printed on thin India paper. (I bought *War and Peace* because *Time* magazine said it was the greatest novel ever written.)

Aylmer Maude's *War and Peace*, in its original maroon and cream wrapper, has accompanied me through half a century's moves from continent to continent. I have a sentimental relation with it—not with Tolstoy's *War and Peace*, that vast construct of words and ideas, but with the object that emerged from the printing house of Richard Clay and Sons in 1952 and was shipped from the warehouse of Oxford University Press somewhere in London to the press's distribution agent in Cape Town and thence to Juta's bookshop and to me.

This kind of relationship with an author—extremely tenuous and highly indirect, conducted through perhaps a dozen intermediaries—will be less and less possible in the future. Whether such relationships have any value seems to me an open question, as is the question of whether it is better to own a physical copy of a book than to have the power to download an image of its text.

The doubt and dismay I express here is not unrelated to the doubt and dismay you express in your most recent letter about the ways in which sport is being reshaped (repackaged) for television. There still happens to be a confluence of interest between what the media want from the game and what the fans who actually attend games want—the fans want what they are so naive as to call the real thing, not a moving image of it, while the media abhor empty stadiums because an empty stadium spells death for the spectacle—but that doesn't mean the business interests that own sports really care about fans except as consumers. If they can find a way of filling seats with holographic images, my guess is they will do so.

Your dismay and my dismay: the shared dismay of two aging gents at the way the world is going. How does one escape the entirely risible fate of turning into Gramps, the old codger who, when he embarks on one of his "Back in my time" discourses, makes the children roll their eyes in silent despair? The world is going to hell in a handbasket, said my father, and his father before him, and so on back to Adam. If the world has really been going to hell all these years, shouldn't it have arrived there by now? When I look around, what I see doesn't seem like hell to me.

But what is the alternative to griping? Clamping one's lips shut and bearing the affronts?

Yours ever,

John

Dear Gramps,

I have always wondered how the world, which is very large, can fit into something as small as a handbasket. To deepen my confusion, I'm not even sure I know what a handbasket is. Aren't all baskets in fact *hand*baskets, and if they are, isn't the prefix *hand* wholly unnecessary? We should probably say: "The world is going to hell in a basket," although that sounds even worse, doesn't it? What should contain the world as we watch it descend into hell? A locomotive? An automobile? A cardboard envelope? Or perhaps something so small that it can't even be seen. A single atom?

The truth is, griping can be fun, and as rapidly aging gentlemen, seasoned observers of the human comedy, wise gray heads who have seen it all and are surprised by nothing, I feel it is our duty to gripe and scold, to attack the hypocrisies, injustices, and stupidities of the world we live in. Let the young roll their eyes when we speak. Let the not so young ignore what we say. We must carry on with utmost vigilance, scorned prophets crying into the wilderness—for just because we know we are fighting a losing battle, that doesn't mean we should abandon the fight.

Yours in friendship,

Paul

September 4, 2010

Dear Paul,

Dorothy and I leave for France this week. We'll be meeting old cycling friends in Montpellier and going on a bike tour, hoping that it is not too late in the year for pleasant weather. I'll have intermittent e-mail access but no fax access.

I looked up going to hell in a handbasket in a dictionary of idioms. It gave "going to hell in a handcart" as a variant but didn't explain what a handbasket was. All baskets aren't handbaskets. There is such a thing as a bushel basket. And now for the interesting bit. Each market town in medieval France had its own bushel basket, and therefore its own opinion of what constituted a bushel of wheat. You would talk of an Orléans bushel and a Lyons bushel. For grain dealers it was maddening. One of the arguments for enforcing a single authority over the whole country was to standardize weights and measures. Presumably the same held, mutatis mutandis, for other countries. More than that memory will not deliver up. No idea of dates.

Warmest wishes,

John

Dear John,

I envy your trip to Montpellier—and admire your courage in climbing aboard yet another plane for yet another ultradistance flight. The weather at this time of year should be perfect. The intense dry heat of the summer gone, the chill of winter still a long way off.

Why don't you write me a letter about it when you return? The pleasures and hardships of cycling. We have written so much about watching sports, it might be helpful to have an account of one of us actually doing something.

Apropos: last week a friend of mine sent me a short book published by an American sports writer in 1955, A *Day in the Bleachers,* which recounts a single baseball game in scrupulous detail, the first game of the 1954 World Series between the New York Giants and the Cleveland Indians at the now vanished Polo Grounds, which happened to be the game in which Willie Mays made his historic catch. A charming and entertaining book, which I thoroughly enjoyed. One of the complaints of the writer: too many people were coming to the stadium with transistor radios and listening to the play-by-play account as the actual game was unfolding before their eyes. He felt disgusted by the introduction of technology into what he felt should be a pure and unmediated human experience. Fifty-six years ago, and yet almost identical to the objections voiced about the jumbo TVs in stadiums today.

Thank you so much for your comments on bushel baskets. We have such things in America, of course, which are usually small enough to be lifted by one person, but the baskets used for storing grain in ancient times, yes, they must have been fairly enormous. The only slang dictionary I have (the British one compiled by Eric Partridge) has much to say about the word basket*:

1. In the 18th century, basket! was a cry directed, in cock-pits, at persons unable, or unwilling, to pay their debts. Such persons were suspended in a basket over the cock-pits. (Looking up cock-pits, I find: 1. A Dissenters' meeting-house. 2. The Treasury, the Privy Council.)

2. Basketed: left out in the cold, misunderstood, nonplussed.

3. Polite term for "bastard." "That basket So-and-so . . ."

4. Disrespectful term for an elderly woman. "Silly old basket . . ."

5. Go to the basket: to be imprisoned.

6. Basket-making: sexual intercourse.

7. "Grin like a basket of chips": to grin broadly.

8. Basket of oranges: a pretty woman—derived from Australian miners' slang for the discovery of gold nuggets in the gold fields.

9. Basket-scrambler: One who lives on charity.

And then, of course, there is the American term "basket case"—which both of us are all too familiar with.

Have a wonderful trip—and write when you return.

With love to you and Dorothy,

Paul

* From the *Dictionary of English Slang*.

October 21, 2010

Dear Paul,

Dorothy and I are back from France, and I am halfway through the purgatory of readjusting to Australian time. I snatch at sleep whenever it offers itself, day or night, but for the most part I wander around the house feeling like death.

The cycling tour was a great success. The weather was perfect, the five-member party got along famously, and the landscape was unfailingly interesting. I'm talking about the Cévennes—I am not sure whether you know the region.

I suppose I could say I wouldn't mind going back and doing it again; but at my age going back anywhere and doing anything again begins to feel a bit hypothetical.

I should have kept a diary, but I didn't. There was a lot of hill climbing, some of which tested me to the limit. Climbing hills on a bicycle can be a great school of stoicism, if stoicism is what you are after. I'm not prepared to believe that all that effort, all that suffering, teaches one nothing.

In the pile of mail waiting for my return was a long letter from a woman in France. It is the third letter I have had from her in the course of some fifteen years. I have never met her. Her letters run to twenty or thirty pages each, in an attractively flowing cursive handwriting. They are for the most part about herself, her loneliness, her troubled relations with her grown-up son, her difficult relations with men, and about me, that is to say about the image of me she has constructed from my books.

She is well aware that the *vous* to whom she writes is a construct and may bear little relation to my own construct of myself. Now and again she opens the possibility that I will respond and make contact with her. She likes to think we are soul mates of a kind. But she does not fantasize much about our meeting, or at least does not write about it.

Sometimes she seems to be saying that what she is doing is supplying me with a character (herself) to use in some future book. In other words, she seems to be asking me to give her new life by making her into a heroine.

She is by no means a fool. She is able to maintain a nice distance from her need for another life without denying the validity of that need. But there is something she does not see, and will not see, I suspect, unless I tell her, which I certainly won't do (a) because I don't want to open the floodgates of a proper correspondence, and (b) because it would be too cruel—namely that I am not much interested in her thoughts about herself or about me or about life, that she would stand a better chance of becoming the heroine of a book if she would send me a long, minutely detailed description of a typical day in her life.

There is a point to be made here about novelists and the sources of their inspiration, namely that half the time (most of the time?) they aren't interested in fathoming the unique, individual essence of their model, just in taking over some interesting, usable quirk or feature of her: the way the hair curls over her ear, the way she pronounces the word "Divine!," the way her toes turn in as she walks.

As for me, I must say I prefer making up characters from scratch. It feels more like the real thing that way.

All the best,

John

Dear John,

I'm glad you made it back in one piece—if only barely. Struggling up a mountain on a bicycle is not an activity I would relish, and when I think of how much you must have suffered, my heart swells with compassion for you. I doubt that sort of pain would teach me anything, and I admire you for having the guts to push yourself to the limit and feel that all that effort is to some purpose. Mental stoicism, yes. Emotional stoicism, yes. But self-inflicted physical torture is altogether mystifying to me. My idea of a good bicycle trip would be to pedal through the lowlands of Holland or the flatlands of the American Midwest—with the wind at my back.

I have not been to the Cévennes—but to areas very close by, and I have experienced the intense beauty of those landscapes. There are few better places in the world, I feel, perhaps none. Some painful climbs up some difficult hills, then, but also the pleasure of breathing that air in the welcoming post-summer weather, and suddenly the whole adventure becomes worthwhile . . .

I have received some long letters from readers, but never twenty or thirty pages long, and certainly not three long letters from the same person. Again and again, however, people have either written to me or said to me: you should write my story—or my mother's story, or my grandfather's story. I have never known how to respond. Writing a novel is all generated from within, and I can't imagine how a novelist could ever appropriate a stranger's life into a book. I'm with you: making up people from scratch feels more like the real thing.

But we do borrow from life, there's no question about that. Personal experiences (often microscopic ones) or the experiences of people who are close to us. In one of my early books (*The Locked Room*), I went so far as to use a real person as a character and call him by his real name—a friend of mine from my days in Paris, Ivan Wyshnegradsky, an eighty-year-old Russian composer of quarter-tone music. He was dead by the time I wrote the book, and I wanted to honor his memory by bringing him to life in a work of fiction—even if all the events I recount about him were based on fact. In my soon to be published *Sunset Park*, the scene at the beginning of the second section is taken directly from life: December 31, 2008, when Siri and I attended the funeral of the daughter of friends of ours who had committed suicide in Venice earlier that month. I could cite other examples as well, but even more interesting is the use of historical figures in novels. You did it with Dostoyevsky in *The Master of Petersburg*, and on a much smaller scale I did it with Tesla (*Moon Palace*) and Dizzy Dean (*Mr. Vertigo*). And then, too, we have both used *ourselves* as characters in novels (*Summertime, City of Glass*), even if those selves are not precise representations of who we are outside the pages of those books.

On the other hand—and here I can speak only about myself—there is no instance in which I have taken a real person, changed that person's name, and then put him or her into a novel. I mean the whole person, a character with identical physical properties, an identical history, and a soul identical to the model. Many novelists have done this (i.e., the notorious roman à clef), but I am not one of them.

And yet, as you so aptly put it, we are constantly stealing interesting, usable quirks or features. The shape of a man's eyebrows, the timbre of someone's laugh, the birthmark on a woman's neck. All the rest seems to spring forth unbidden from the deepest recesses of the imagination.

Another aspect of novel writing (and novel reading) that I often think about is the question of space. As a reader, I sometimes find myself struggling to situate the action, to understand the geography of a story. This might have something to do with my impoverished visual imagination. Rather than project myself into the fictive settings the author has described (a small town in Mississippi, a street in Tokyo, a bedroom in an eighteenth-century English house), I tend to put the characters in places I am personally familiar with. I hadn't realized I was guilty of this habit until I read *Pride and Prejudice* in my early twenties (a book with almost no physical descriptions) and found myself "seeing" the characters in the house where I lived as a boy. An astonishing revelation. But how can you see a room in a book if the author doesn't tell you what is in it? You therefore make up your own room, or graft the scene onto a remembered room. This explains why each reader of a novel reads a different book from every other reader of that novel. It is an active engagement, and each mind is continually producing its own images.

When I write, however, it seems that the process is reversed. The spaces in my novels are entirely concrete for me. Every street, every house, every room is vividly real in my mind—

even if I say little or nothing about it. I might not mention where the sofa is, but I know exactly where it is positioned in relation to the other furniture. It is all about grounding the imagination in the specific, I think, which allows one to believe—or delude oneself into believing—that the things one is writing about are actually happening.

I am curious to know if any of this resonates with you— both as reader and writer.

With friendliest good thoughts,

Paul

P.S.: There is a highly entertaining American film about cycling from the late seventies—*Breaking Away*—which you might want to take a look at. A terrific sense of place (Bloomington, Indiana), which is rare in American films.

P.P.S.: Paulo Branco was in town last week and said he would like to have us on the jury again next year—a jury composed exclusively of writers. I am more than game.

Dear Paul,

You mention that Paulo Branco might again require us for jury duty in Estoril. That would be nice. November is the month of the year, as I remember.

I know the film *Breaking Away*—in fact, I think I own a copy. It becomes a bit formulaic toward the end—the working-class hero racing against the preppy students—but I agree, the locale and social environment are splendidly evoked.

When it comes to cycling up hills, be assured, I take as little pleasure in it as you would. As for the sense of achievement that is supposed to accompany arrival at the crest, my experience is that it is much overrated. What drives people to run or cycle long distances remains a bit of a mystery to me. Nevertheless, thousands of people do it every day, all over the world.

At the risk of seeming precious, I would link it to the question, Why write? Samuel Johnson said, in effect, that one would be a fool if one did not expect payment for one's labor. But I find myself spending hours polishing pieces of prose to a sheen well past the standard for publication and hence payment.

I suppose I would excuse myself by saying, "I'm not the kind of person who puts defective prose out into the world," as I would say, "I'm not the kind of person who gets off his bicycle and walks" (who gets off his bicycle and walks *even when no one is looking*). That, I think, is the interesting part. Few readers are going to appreciate what goes into getting a paragraph exactly right. No one is going to see if you get off your bike and walk, or for that matter if you give up and freewheel back down the hill. *But that's not me, that's not my idea of myself!*

You write about knowing precisely where the fictional sofa is in your fictional room, even though no one in your book is going to sit on it or even spare it a glance. I think I may be a little less thorough. The room in which my fictional action takes place is a pretty bare place, an empty cube, in fact; I import a sofa only if it turns out to be needed (if someone is going to sit on it or look at it), and after that the dresser with the set of cutlery in the top left-hand drawer without which we cannot have the butter knife with which the heroine is going to butter her toast.

At the time he was teaching literature at Cornell, I understand Vladimir Nabokov used to require his students to draw floor plans on the basis of the information supplied by the novel they were reading in class. The weak Nabokovian thesis would be that the novelist should not provide internally contradictory data (a carpet that is red on one page and blue on another). The strong thesis would be that there should be enough data in the text for the student to draw plans and diagram the physical movements of the characters, scene by scene.

I see some similarity between the strong thesis and the received wisdom of playwriting or screenwriting classes that the writer should be able to jot down the entire back story of each of his characters, if only as an aid to the actors, even if those back stories will in no form emerge in the film or play itself.

If this is the industry standard, I fail. For none of the adult characters of my books do I have much idea of, for instance, what sort of childhood they had, just as I have not the faintest idea what is going to happen to them after the last page.

Since I last wrote, you have had congressional elections in the U.S., and the Republicans have resurged in force. I won't ask you to explain. But this is beginning to look like an interesting moment in history (and I don't just mean U.S. history).

Since about 1970, a pretty mean vision has been propagated and encouraged and allowed to take over the direction of the planet, a vision of human beings as machines of self-interest and of economic activity as a contest of all against all for material spoils (economy: properly the *nomos* of the *oikos*, the regulation of the household).

As a consequence a debased notion of what constitutes political life has come to prevail, and has in turn given rise to a pretty contemptuous view of what constitutes the practice of politics. Thus the same politicians who did nothing to counter the mean vision of social life get to feel the fury and contempt, the furious contempt, of voters who see them as little more than machines of self-interest themselves. The word "trust" has lost all purchase. If today a politician were to utter on a public platform the words, "I ask you to trust me," he would be laughed down, no matter how sincerely he meant it.

Yours in dark times,

John

November 12, 2010

Dear John,

Yes, the midterm American election results were unfortunate—but after an all-out propaganda assault on Obama and the Democrats by the right and the far right for the past two years, not unexpected. The time is dark, certainly, the news is grim, certainly, but I try to ward off terminal depression by taking the long view, the historical view, and console myself with the fact that we have been here before. Not just in the recent past—the right-wing election blitzes of 1994 and 1980, for example—but the late forties and early fifties as well, when the Republicans, who had been out of the White House since 1932, grew ever more insane in their attacks on Roosevelt, the New Deal, and "un-American" left-wing thinking, which brought us the Korean War, McCarthy, and the ideological hysteria of the cold war. Before that: the horrors of World War II and the miseries of the Great Depression. Before that: the ferocious, frequently violent battles between capital and labor. I could keep going back, all the way to the founding of the republic. A strange, pendular motion, oscillating between those who believe in American exceptionalism (we, not the Jews, are the chosen people, n'est-ce pas?), unfettered capitalism, the dog-eat-dog mentality of every man for himself, and the others, who believe in what you and I would call a just society, who honestly believe that human beings are responsible for one another. Today, one group has all the answers; tomorrow, the other group kicks them out. In the big scheme, there has been a certain measure of progress (the abolition of slavery, social security benefits, civil rights legislation, legalized abortion), but progress always comes slowly in this too large, too fractious country. Three inches forward, two inches back; three inches forward, five inches back; two inches forward, one inch back.

Much as I hate to admit it, however, this is not a particularly terrible time for the Western world. A ridiculous time, perhaps, a frustrating time, but by no means one of the worst. Witches are not being burned at the stake, French Catholics and Protestants are not tearing out each other's throats, America is not fighting a civil war, millions of Europeans are not dying in mud-filled trenches or concentration camps. Hitler is dead, Stalin is dead, Franco is dead. The monsters of the twentieth century are all gone, and if pygmies tend to be in power now throughout the West, far better to laugh at pygmies than to cringe from murdering tyrants.

But yes, America is a sad place to be right now. So many problems to be dealt with, and for the next two years nothing will be done about them, which will only make the problems worse. And then the battle will begin all over again. Meanwhile, I sit here in Brooklyn watching the great carnival of stupidity that has become our public life and shake my head, hoping the pendulum will eventually swing in the other direction.

The "mean vision" you talk about has been with us a lot longer than since 1970, I'm afraid. And contrary to the view I held when I was young—that people vote out of economic self-interest—I have now come to feel that many voters' choices are entirely irrational—or ideological, even if that ideology goes *against* their economic well-being. In 1984, during Reagan's reelection campaign, I was going somewhere in a Brooklyn car service. The driver, who had been a welder at the Brooklyn Navy Yard, had lost his job when the union he belonged to was crushed by management. I said to him: "You can thank Reagan for that—the greatest union-busting president in history." And he replied: "Maybe so, but I'm voting for him anyway." "Why in the world would you do that?" I asked. His answer: "Because I don't want to see the fucking Commies take over South America."

An indelible moment in my political education. It was men like this, I imagine, who voted Hitler into power in 1933.

To return to reading and writing for a moment, in light of your very interesting comments about empty cubes, Nabakov's floor plans, and the "back stories" of characters in plays and movies. You talk about your spatial sense as a writer, but I'm also curious to know what you "see" in your head when you read a novel or short story—or, better yet, a fairy tale. If you read the following: "Once upon a time, there was an old woman who lived with her daughter in a hut at the edge of a dark wood," what images do you conjure up for yourself, if any? Not much is given here. No names, no ages, no precise place, no physical descriptions, and yet somehow, for reasons that are entirely mysterious to me, I myself tend to fill in the blanks. Not in any elaborate way, perhaps, but enough to imagine a short, bulky woman with an apron around her waist, to imagine a thin adolescent girl with long brown hair and a pale complexion, and to imagine smoke rising out of the chimney of the hut. Does the mind abhor a vacuum? Is there a need to flesh out what is vague and formless, to concretize the action, or can you content yourself with the words on the page, in and of themselves, and if so, what happens to you when you read those words?

No, I didn't mean to imply that *Breaking Away* is a cinematic masterpiece. Just that it is the only film I have seen that pays so much attention to cycling—and that I found it amusing. Of course, the triumphant race at the end is Hollywood claptrap. But the final, final shot of the film is genuinely funny—when the boy, who for months had pretended to be an Italian, meets a pretty French girl on campus, and then shouts out to his bewildered father: "Bonjour, papa!"

Something to ponder. In the past few weeks, I have done roughly a dozen interviews with American journalists about *Sunset Park*, which has just been published. Many of them, in particular the female journalists (all of them female journalists, now that I think of it), are shocked, even scandalized, by the affair of my twenty-eight-year-old character with his seventeen-year-old love. "Underage sex" seems to set off every alarm bell in contemporary American culture. On the other hand, when I talked to journalists about *Invisible*, almost no one mentioned the incest between brother and sister. Quite frankly, I am stumped.

Any thoughts?

With big hugs to you and Dorothy,

Paul

Dear Paul,

"Two inches forward, one inch back"—that's the phrase you use to describe social progress in your country, a country which, inasmuch as it is a world-hegemonic power, is in an important sense my country too, and everyone else's on the planet, but with the proviso that the rest of us don't get to take part in its political processes.

My own somewhat jaundiced view, as a lifelong member of the class of the ruled, is that it is naive to look to our rulers to conduct us to a better future. They have more important fish of their own to fry. Therefore so long as they settle among themselves the problem of peaceful succession, I will make no further demands on them. By the problem of succession I mean simply passing of power from one of them to the next without subjecting the populace to violence.

One has only to look at states that haven't solved the problem of succession to realize what an achievement that is, and conversely what misery it is to live in a country in which contenders resort to arms to win power.

So two cheers for the United States on that score.

I suppose that the stability of the U.S. comes largely from the reverence with which you Americans have been taught (and have learned) to regard your foundational documents. Which raises interesting questions about fundamentalism. As I understand it, there are people in your country who believe that the Constitution and Bill of Rights mean one thing and one thing only, while other people believe that these documents need to be reinterpreted from time to time in the light of changed historical circumstances. This difference on the issue of interpretation (what a written text means or can be said to mean) closely mirrors the theological difference between Christian fundamentalists and their progressive opponents, and no doubt differences within other text-based religions like Judaism and Islam.

I don't know what your opinions are on interpretation and the limits of interpretation. My own feeling is that the spectacle of scholars (or judges) trying to tease out what two-thousand-year-old texts have to say about stem cell research is more than a little comical. When we come to modern times, I do feel that the failure of the Founding Fathers of the United States, back in the eighteenth century, to spell out unambiguously what they meant when they asserted the right of citizens to bear arms was no less than culpable; and, considering the hundreds of thousands of people who have been killed over the years as a direct consequence of literalist interpretations of that statute, successive political administrations in the United States have been culpable too for not having the resolve to scrap the statute and replace it with more specific wording.

A comment from Nietzsche (*Twilight of the Idols*) that I have just come across: "How is freedom measured in individuals as well as in nations? According to the resistance which has to be overcome, according to the pains it costs to remain *uppermost*. The highest type of free man would have to be sought where the greatest resistance is continually to be overcome." One corollary: even if one may, in theory, be born free, one's freedom soon wears off. Another corollary: there is unlikely to be such a place as the land of the free.

In your last letter you push forward the discussion of fictional spaces, asking what I see before my inner eye when I read in a book that there was an old woman who lived with her daughter in a hut at the edge of the forest. Compared with you, I seem to have a pretty paltry visual imagination. In the normal process of reading, I don't believe I "see" anything at all. It is only when you come along and demand a report that I retrospectively assemble a rudimentary old woman in my mind's eye, and a daughter, and a hut, and a forest.

What I do seem to have, in place of visual imagery, is what I vaguely call aura or tonality. When my mind goes back to a particular book that I know, I seem to summon up a unique aura, which of course I can't put into words without in effect rewriting the book.

You confess you are stumped when you try to understand why critics don't complain about incest between brother and sister (in *Invisible*) but are outraged by sex between a man of twenty-eight and a girl (a woman?) of seventeen (in *Sunset Park*).

I am stumped too—particularly since in the latter case the intimacies are so discreetly represented. Fundamentally baffling is the question of what kind of historical age we live in: a puritan age or a permissive age. For it seems to have features of both. On the one hand parents don't object when their sixteen-year-old daughter brings home a boy for the night. They may even offer breakfast to the sated couple the next morning. On the other hand, a grown man who snaps a photograph of a child wearing a swimsuit on the beach finds himself in the lockup.

My tentative hypothesis is that the temper of our times is hostile to desire and wants to punish it. At the same time, however, we are not prepared to punish children, who are by definition blameless. Therefore, a redoubled punitiveness gets directed at the adult who desires a child.

A Freudian would focus on the question of why we have stopped punishing children, and in particular have abandoned corporal chastisement, which used to be the norm but is now virtually tabooed. My guess is that the Freudian would spot a connection between the increasing sexualization of quite young children and the sexual or sexualized coloring that corporal punishment of children inevitably takes on in these circumstances. The intolerable logic would go something like: This child is trying to seduce me. But if I punish her for it I am giving in to her seduction. So what do I do next?

There was an interesting case in Australia a year or two ago. A respected photographer had an exhibition which included photographs of a nude model (female) aged (I believe) twelve. Prompted by vigilante groups, the police closed down the exhibition. The prime minister, Kevin Rudd, was asked in the course of an interview what he thought of the photographs (which had of course been spread on the Internet). For whatever motive—probably he thought it would win him votes—he pronounced the photographs "disgusting" and wondered aloud why we couldn't leave children alone to be children.

There are many things that could be said about this response, the kind of response only to be expected from a politician nowadays who is attentive to public opinion. One would be that it assumes that if we are naked we are sexual, i.e., that the naked, the nude, and the sexual are more or less the same thing.

I remember, a few years ago, writing an essay on pornography in which, as what I thought of as a winning rhetorical move, a reductio ad absurdum, I asked aloud whether we were going to require filmmakers to certify that the actors they used in sex scenes were in no case minors. And, lo and behold, filmmakers are today required to sign declarations of precisely that kind.

Warmest wishes,

John

Dear John,

You ask if I have any opinion on interpretation or the limits
of interpretation, and the first thought that comes to mind (my
dim-witted, associative, hyperactive mind) is a passage I read
many years ago in an English translation of selected portions
of the Talmud. Several rabbis are discussing the possible circumstances that might prevent a person from reciting his daily
prayers. One rabbi mentions shit as an impediment. If you find
yourself standing next to a pile of shit, it would be blasphe-
mous to invoke the name of God, wouldn't it? The other rabbis agree. But what is to be done? Go somewhere else, of
course. But what if you are unable to go somewhere else? One
rabbi suggests covering the shit with a cloth or a piece of paper. As long as the shit is out of sight, he says, you can proceed
as if it weren't there. The other rabbis agree. Then the youngest rabbi brings up a vexing point. What if the shit is on the
sole of your shoe—and you aren't aware of it? Are you allowed
to pray or not? The next sentence, I remember, was the following: "To this they had no reply."

Meaning, I suppose, that interpretation can go just so far,
and sooner or later you will come upon a question that cannot
be answered. If you are compelled to give an answer (as judges
are compelled to), it will necessarily be arbitrary, that is to say,
personal, a product of who and what you are, a reflection of
your private beliefs about how the world should be run. In the
case of the aforementioned rabbis, I can easily imagine the
conversation continuing—although thankfully, and beauti-

fully, it does not. A liberal-minded rabbi would tell his young colleague to go ahead with his prayers. As long as he doesn't know there is shit on the sole of his shoe, how can he be held accountable? God will understand and forgive him. But a fundamentalist rabbi would say just the opposite. Shit is shit, he would argue, the law is the law, and since it is forbidden to pray in the presence of shit, you would be committing an offense against God if you recited your prayers with shit on the sole of your shoe.

To go on a little further with this, since you talk about the peaceful transition of power in the United States and the reverence of Americans for their "foundational documents" . . . You have lived here long enough and often enough to understand American life as well as I do, but at the same time you stand apart from this place (and why shouldn't you?) in ways that are not possible for me. You look at yourself as one of the "ruled," and given the mischief America has created around the world these past umpteen years, a certain dose of skepticism about the American project is not unwarranted, is in fact perfectly understandable. I feel that skepticism too, but I am also of this place and deeply attached to it, and whenever America blunders (far too often), my pain is intense. Never more terribly (if we are on the subjects of government succession, interpretation of texts, fundamentalism, and foundational documents) than with the Supreme Court decision following the 2000 presidential election, the Gore versus Bush fiasco. I'm sure you remember what happened. To me, the remarkable thing about it was how quickly—and eagerly—supposedly fundamentalist interpreters of the law were willing to betray their so-called beliefs and convictions to put their man in office. One rarely gets to see intellectual frauds in action on such a large stage, and the hypocrisy of what I witnessed during those weeks has left me feeling bitter, still bitter ten years after the fact. So much for our reverence for America's foundational documents. In the end, ideas count for little or nothing when it comes to the struggle for political power. The Supreme Court pulled off a coup d'état for the Republican Party under the guise of perfect legality.

Gore won. But his victory was not decisive enough to prevent that victory from being stolen from him, and one of the reasons why he didn't have an overwhelming number of votes, perhaps the only reason, was that Bill Clinton got caught with his pants down. (A joke of the day: Why does Bill Clinton wear underpants? Answer: To keep his ankles warm.) Again, no need to rehash the facts, but here we come to the last part of your letter and your assertion (your correct assertion) that we are living in a punitive time when it comes to sexual matters. Tremendous license on the one hand, yes, but also the same old puritanical judgments that have been with us since the first colonists set foot in New England. Without the Clinton sex scandal, probably no Bush. And with no Bush, perhaps no 9/11—which would mean no Iraq, no Afghanistan, no illegal torture. For want of a nail . . .

All the points you raise in your letter seem to come together in this one dismal story.

Must run, but I wanted to dash off a few words to you before leaving. I'll be back in New York on the sixteenth. In the meantime, I offer you an American military expression from

World War II, which I recently came across for the first time: FUBAR. (Translation: fucked up beyond all recognition.) Not bad, eh?

> Warmest best,
>
> Paul

Dear Paul,

I stumbled on a little thought experiment the other day that has alternately been troubling and amusing me.

I was reflecting on my situation in life, on how I got to be where I am (namely in the suburbs of a small city in Australia), and on the various accidents, including the accident of my birth—being born to particular parents on a particular day—that led to my being not only where I am but who I am. It occurred to me that it was all too easy to contemplate a world in which this fellow John Maxwell Coetzee, born February 9, 1940, was not present and had never been present, or else had lived a completely different life, perhaps not even a human life; but at the next instant it also occurred to me that it was impossible to contemplate a world in which *I* was not present and had never been present.

I tried the trick again, thinking first the one thought (the world without JMC), then the other (the world without *me*), and again it worked. The first was easy to think, the second impossible.

The simple logical conclusion would seem to be that the equation "I = JMC" is false. And indeed one's intuitions support this conclusion. I imagine that you find the equation "I = PA" equally false.

But have you ever before seen the falsity of the equation demonstrated so neatly?

Dorothy and I set out tomorrow morning for India, on our first visit there. Preparations for the visit have involved an unusual amount of shit—I mean literal shit. We had to have inoculations against diseases transmitted through shit (hepatitis, cholera), we have been warned from all quarters to wash our hands at frequent intervals and not put food in our mouths that has passed through the (shitty) hands of strangers, and now I read in the *New York Review of Books* blog that while men in India may shit in public without shame, being seen to relieve oneself during daylight hours is unacceptable for Indian women. Hence a wide range of diseases of the urinary tract and bowels among women.

It always comes as a shock to find how elementary the basis is of taboos. For instance, wearing shoes in a mosque and sitting down in a mosque are both taboo. Why? Because the soles of one's shoes have probably trodden in shit (obvious); and because the seat of one's pants is probably soiled too (not so obvious).

Thanks for your last letter (December 3), also featuring shit on shoes.

All the best,

John

January 28, 2011

Dear John,

After months of work and a hundred pages written, I decided to abandon—or put aside—the novel I started in late spring. The book seemed to be spreading out in all directions rather than coming into focus, and I haven't figured out a way to fix it. I have never dropped any project so deep into it—but, in spite of my disappointment, I am convinced I made the right decision. I wonder if anything similar has ever happened to you—and, if so, how you dealt with it.

Tell me about India. A place I have never been to, and about which I know very little.

Five feet of snow in New York this past month—one storm after another. It is turning into one of *those* winters.

> Fondest thoughts—and big hugs to you both,
>
> Paul

March 3, 2011

Dear Paul,

I've been wanting to write to you about India, but then thought I ought to let enough time pass for my thoughts to settle and perhaps grow more mature, more interesting. Now I find that they aren't growing at all, merely settling, so there is no reason for procrastinating any longer.

I was invited to the Jaipur literary festival, which I thought I would use as an entrée to a tour, if not of India then at least of Rajasthan. If Rajasthan worked, I thought, I might at some future date explore another part of the country, perhaps Kerala, with a little more confidence.

About the Jaipur festival I had mixed feelings. I had heard it was large and noisy, which didn't recommend it to me. On the other hand, there would surely be sympathetic souls there, Indian and foreign, and I would have time to consult with them about good and bad, advisable and inadvisable, ways of seeing the country.

I don't think I distinguished myself at the festival. I was determined not to subject myself to the rounds of public questioning that have become a standard feature of festivals nowadays. Interrogation is not a medium I do well in. I am too brief in my responses, where brevity (clippedness) is all too easily misread as a sign of irritation or anger. So I announced that I was simply going to read a piece of fiction. This was what I did. The fiction wasn't amusing (it was about life and death and the soul), so it was probably a bad choice for that kind of occasion. The audience response: respectful but puzzled.

Anyway, after five days the festival was over and I had gathered no particular wisdom from sporadic conversations about how to approach India. Worse, I had picked up a low fever which left me feeling lethargic most of the time.

So Dorothy and I set off on a one-week, fixed-price tour of Rajasthan in a car with a driver named Rakesh. Rakesh drove us from Jaipur to Pushkar to Jodhpur to Udaipur to Bundi and back to Jaipur, and when the tour was over put us on a plane out of the country.

I suppose I could at this point list the sights along the way that made an impression on me. But I suspect you will want more from a letter than that. So I will limit myself to two observations on what I saw, and then perhaps reflect on the question of why I am such a poor reporter, not only on India but on all of life.

My first observation was that this was the first country I had visited where human beings and animals seem to have worked out a decent modus vivendi. The range of animal species I actually observed was limited—cows, pigs, dogs, monkeys—but I have no reason to think that only these animals are accepted into the human sphere. I saw no sign of cruel treatment, no sign even of impatience, though the cows wander in among the very busy traffic and hold people up.

It is commonplace that cows are worshipped in India. But worship seems to me the wrong word. Relations between people and animals are much more mundane than that: a simple tolerance and acceptance of an animal's way of being, even when it intrudes among men.

Behind this observation lies my experience in Africa, where animals are also omnipresent but where an unthinking cruelty toward them is common, an attitude of contempt toward them as a lower form of life.

Paul Auster and J. M. Coetzee

My other observation concerns poverty, and again the contrast with Africa was at the back of my mind. "The poor" in India do indeed seem to be living perilously close to subsistence level, to be scraping a bare existence from day to day. But the more I saw of this bare existence, the more I was impressed by the reservoir of practical skills people were drawing on, as well as by their sheer industriousness. Whether one was looking at men chipping building blocks out of quarried sandstone or at vendors preparing food at the roadside, these were dextrous people with what I can only call intelligent hands who, in another kind of economic setup, could be prosperous artisans. In other words, there seemed to me to be vast human resources that are only very partially tapped at present.

And now we come to the observer himself, the man who emerges from a two-week immersion in a foreign culture (and a foreign civilization) with nothing to show for it save a handful of trite and rather abstract observations. Why am I incapable of travel writing in all its splendor—of the vivid evocation of strange sights and sounds? I know you will say, "But surely you are in good company. Where are the vivid evocations of strange sights and sounds in Kafka? Where are they in Beckett?" But is it good enough to rely on that kind of consolation? Isn't it plain old inadequacy that one is exhibiting—an inadequate response to the beauty and generosity of the world? What is praiseworthy in trying to turn a native poverty into a virtue?

Questions, questions.

Yours ever,

John

March 7, 2011

Dear Paul,

I have heard from the organizers of events in Canada that they have got as far as making hotel reservations for us. Excellent. I'm looking forward very much to spending some time with you. A pity Siri can't be there.

Dorothy will be coming along—she will be presenting a paper at an academic conference at Queen's University at more or less the same time.

I'm sorry to hear you found yourself (in January) having to abandon a project into which you had obviously put a lot of work. But these investments are never wholly lost, are they? A page or two, an idea here and there, can surely be rescued, and (to drift into horticultural metaphor) may perhaps in time put down roots of its own.

I have abandoned projects in the past, though my native tendency is to push on too long, perhaps, and too doggedly with a no-hoper.

What interests me at the present juncture is the question of how and when failing power will announce itself. One can't go on writing forever; and one doesn't want to sign off with an embarrassingly bad product of one's dotage. How does one detect that one just doesn't have it in one anymore to do justice to a subject?

All good wishes,

John

Dear John,

Happy to receive your latest—your two latest—and to know that you are back in one piece.

The fact is, travel writing tends to bore me, and even films about exotic places—which theoretically should grab you by the seat of your pants—have always left me cold. I remember the travelogues they used to show between the cartoons and the feature when I was a boy—works of unspeakable dullness that would send me rushing out to the concession stand within two minutes.

Not that I haven't taken pleasure in certain classics of the genre—Herodotus, Marco Polo, Sir John Mandeville, Saint Brendan, Columbus, Cabeza de Vaca—so many of them filled with lies and outlandish inventions—along with some nineteenth-century books of real literary merit: Doughty's *Travels in Arabia Deserta*, Parkman's *The Oregon Trail*, and Powell's *Exploration of the Colorado River and Its Canyons*—but the travel-writing boom of the eighties never said much of anything to me, and when you get right down to it, I much prefer the imaginary anthropologies of Calvino's *Invisible Cities* or Henri Michaux's prose poem "I am writing to you from a far-off country" or even Cyrano de Bergerac's seventeenth-century account of his trip to the moon—works of pure fantasy that seem to say more about human life than any book or article of down-to-earth reportage.

You lament the poverty of your skills as an observer of "strange sights and sounds," but you are not a reporter—neither by training nor temperament—and the kind of attentiveness you bring to your experiences is of a different order from that of a journalist. The newspaperman and travel writer concentrate on the surfaces of things. Their job is to create word pictures for their readers, to look closely at each visual fact that presents itself to them and turn it into a captivating phrase or sentence, but you are looking at several things at once, at everything at once, and trying to make sense of what you see—that is, trying to synthesize the disparate facts into an observation that will encompass more than just the surfaces of things, that will pierce through to the inner depths. I was therefore grateful to you for your comments about the relations between human beings and animals in India (which I have never heard from anyone else) and the industry of what you call "intelligent hands." Much better to read those things than to be told the color of the cups poor people drink from.

March 10

Fractured, busy days—which prevented me from continuing on the eighth . . .

A word about Canada in September. I know how uncomfortable you feel about "public interrogation," but that seems to be precisely what they want us to do together. The two of us alone on stage with no intermediary, first to give short readings from our work, and then to have some kind of conversation. We should probably figure out beforehand what we want to talk about (in the most general terms, a few major points) and then wing it from there. Some of our remarks will necessarily take the form of questions—each to the other—but not the kind of grilling one associates with traditional interviews. We should be all right, I guess, and if your statements are clipped, what difference does that make? I tend to be rather clipped myself.

The difficulty of understanding current events in distant parts of the world. Except for what is happening in front of my nose here in America, everything I know is filtered through the media (mostly the *New York Times* and the *New York Review of Books*, but also some TV and radio), and the farther away I am from the events in question, the less certain I am about what I know. I can grasp the tawdry farce of the recent Italian scandals (European politics are not alien to me), but when it comes to what is happening in the Middle East, I feel on less solid ground. What we are told in the American press is that spontaneous revolutions have occurred in Tunisia and Egypt, that protest movements have sprung up in several other countries throughout the region, and that the conflict in Libya is quickly devolving into a bloody civil war. To concentrate on Egypt for the moment: it seems that the peaceful uprising was secular in nature, for the most part led by young people in their twenties and thirties—educated young people who are largely unemployed or underemployed because of the malfunctioning society created by years of corruption and dictatorship—and supported by women, civil servants, impoverished workers, and even the military. Everyone praised the extraordinary fervor and dedication of the rebels, and yet now, just weeks later, cracks seem to be forming again, violent confrontations have been growing (most recently between Christians and Muslims), and all in all the situation seems perilously unstable to me. Decades of no true political life, no organized political parties, and no possibility of coherent political opposition have led to a kind of mass hunger for social change, but with no political tools to implement it—which has left the army in control of the country, at least for now. I sense there is a vacuum of power, and when I think about revolutions of the past, that sort of vacuum tends to produce a Napoleon or a Lenin, the brilliant opportunist who steps into the breach and takes control by force. Those are my fears—but what do I really know about what is going on, and what do I really know about the people involved? Next to nothing. Meanwhile, America debates whether we should start dropping bombs on Libya. One shudders to think . . .

With warmest greetings,

Paul

Dear Paul,

You don't use e-mail and (I am pretty sure) you don't carry a mobile phone. I presume that these are principled decisions on your part. I am not at all interested in what they say at a personal level. What intrigues me is what it will mean to be a twenty-first-century person writing fiction from which twenty-first-century tools of communication like the mobile phone are absent.

Before I say any more, be assured that my sympathies are very much on your side. I too have, willy-nilly, become a twenty-first-century person, yet I write books in which people write (and mail) paper letters, books in which the most up-to-date means of communication employed is (now and again) the telephone, which happens to be a nineteenth-century invention.

The presence/absence of mobile phones in one's fictional world is going to be, I suspect, no trivial matter. Why? Because so much of the mechanics of novel writing, past and present, is taken up with making information available to characters or keeping it from them, with getting people together in the same room or holding them apart. If, all of a sudden, everyone has access to more or less everyone else—electronic access, that is—what becomes of all that plotting? In the movies, one is already used to seeing all kinds of little plot routines being invoked to explain why character A can *not* speak to character B (phone left behind in taxi; phone reception blocked by mountains). The default situation has become that, save in extraordinary circumstances, B is always contactable by A.

Is it going to become the norm of the fiction of tomorrow (indeed, of today) that everyone always has access to everyone else, with the corollary that if in a specific fictional world everyone does not have access to everyone else then that fictional world belongs to the past?

One used to be able to get pages and pages out of the non-existence of the telegraph/telephone (yet to be invented) and the consequent need for messages to be borne by hand or even memorized at one end and recited at the other (example: the man who had to race from Marathon to Athens). Are many of the stories that you and I and people like us write doomed to be seen as fictions premised on the nonexistence of the mobile phone, and therefore as quaint?

Think further of what the mobile phone has done to the practice of adultery (the adaptations that adulterers have had to make), and to the practice of deception in general. A contemporary novel of adultery (or a novel of contemporary adultery) would have a quite different mechanics.

Without making a mountain out of a molehill, let me also point to the growing lists of goods and services unavailable to people without mobiles (not nearly as large as the list of goods and services unavailable to people without access to the Internet, but nevertheless . . .). The pressure is definitely on us to have a mobile each—pressure, in effect, to have a number, a code, at which we can be located at all hours of the day and night. When every citizen has such a number, what need will there any longer be for a physical identity document?

Already there are fictions in which mobile phones are used as tracking devices. Some unlucky guy in a turban switches on his mobile, and an instant later is hit by a missile fired from a drone.

With memories of your praise of William Wyler at the back of my mind, I have been watching what films of his I can lay my hands on—in the last couple of weeks, *Mrs. Miniver, The Desperate Hours, The Children's Hour,* and a film based on a Somerset Maugham story, starring Bette Davis, whose title escapes me.

Wyler does everything so efficiently and unobtrusively that one barely notices the authorial hand. I'd like to talk to you about him one day, and hear what, as someone in the business, you admire.

Your comments on the current situation in Egypt seem exactly right. One watches those intelligent, fresh-faced, enthusiastic youngsters on the streets of Cairo telling the television cameras how great it feels to be free, how much they are looking forward to a new Egypt, and one wonders how they will be talking in two or three years, when a new ruling elite will have settled into power.

I keep thinking that it is only in those all too brief interregnums, when one power has been overthrown and the next has yet to install itself, that people have a true taste of liberty—Europe between the eclipse of the Nazis and the arrival of the New Austerity, for example. How rare it is, a chance for the masses to dance in the streets! And how quaint that term, *the masses!*

All the best,

John

Dear John,

Yet another friend has given me an old manual typewriter, in this case an Olivetti Lettera 22 (circa 1958–60), which I have just carried back from Manhattan, where for the past two weeks it was in the hands of a man named Paul Schweitzer, whose Gramercy Office Equipment Co. is *the last place in New York* where typewriters are still repaired. For $275, my new toy was given a complete overhaul, and I am now using it for the first time, taking immense pleasure in the feel of the keyboard and the elegance of its design. Such a nifty, compact piece of machinery—small enough and light enough to serve in the future as a travel typewriter, something I have been without for many years.

Good timing (or strange timing) in light of your recent remarks about cell phones and other forms of digital technology. Yes, all these instruments are now an integral part of daily life, and novelists cannot speak of the contemporary world without acknowledging the existence of these inventions. Although I no longer have a cell phone myself (I owned one briefly, rarely used it, and subsequently gave it to my then teenage daughter, who had lost three phones in the past nine months), I am not so ignorant or stubborn as to want to force my contrarian views on the characters in my books. In my last novel, which is a story set entirely in the Now, cell phones figure in the action, and even though I have also given away my laptop (which I had used for work on a screenplay), computers and the Internet have appeared in other novels I have written in the twenty-first century. I am a realist! I might long for the old days (record stores, palatial movie houses, smoking permitted everywhere), I might feel depressed when I realize that my dinner companions have suddenly stopped talking and are all looking at their cell phones, but however mixed my feelings might be about these wondrous gadgets—which were built in order to bring people together but in fact often drive them apart—I know that this is how the world lives now, and there's nothing I can do but keep up a brave front and try to accept it.

One could, of course, write historical novels. If one were interested in historical novels, that is—which I am not.

The novel of adultery: a lovely term, which brought a smile to my face. No doubt it is more difficult to hide from your spouse when both of you have cell phones. But people sometimes switch off their phones, and sometimes they will receive a call, check to see who has called, and not bother to answer (I have observed this). On the other hand, repeated failure to answer your wife's calls might not be such a good idea if you want to keep your marriage intact—which, I assume, is the aim of all adulterers. And yet I can't believe that adultery is any less prevalent today than it was before everyone had a cell phone in his pocket. It might demand new forms of deviousness—but that would be a challenge most novelists would welcome.

You talk about everyone being available to everyone else, and in a sense that is true—but only in a fragmented, ad hoc sort of way. There are no directories for cell phones. Those fat books listing the numbers of traditional landlines still exist (in a large city like New York, the books are positively obese), but the distribution of cell phone numbers is a private affair. I have your number because you gave it to me, but there is nowhere for me to look it up, no public access to your private number. But once

I do have it, of course, I can contact you anywhere, any time, for the mobile phone (a much better term than the American *cell phone*) goes wherever you go. There are many advantages to this new system (especially in the case of emergencies and accidents), but many disadvantages as well (as in the case of clandestine, adulterous affairs). All in all, probably a wash. Where films are concerned, however, cell phones strike me as a positive step forward. Now that no one is allowed to smoke anymore, they give actors something to do with their hands.

On the subject of film, I'm impressed that you are taking the trouble to look into William Wyler. I can't say that I admire him as much as you think I do (or might have led you to think). Whenever I make an imaginary list of my favorite directors from around the world, or even my favorite American directors, his name is never on it—in fact, never even comes up for consideration. It's true that I have an enormous soft spot for *The Best Years of Our Lives,* which I rank as his finest film and one of the top Hollywood films ever made, but nothing else of his comes close to it. There are others that I like, of course, but not necessarily the ones you have seen lately—although, if the title of the Bette Davis film is *The Letter,* then you have seen what is probably one of his best after *The Best. . . .* The other two that I think are extremely good were both adapted from American novels: *Dodsworth,* 1936 (Sinclair Lewis) and *The Heiress,* 1949 (Henry James, *Washington Square*). He is a beautiful stylist, a terrifically talented director of actors (many impressive performances), visually stimulating (especially in the films shot by Gregg Toland—a genius who died of a heart attack at forty-four), but someone so good at his craft that I rarely feel the mark of something personal, that indefinable something that separates the great from the very good. André Bazin, the well-known French film critic, made a big fuss about Wyler's importance in *Cahiers du Cinéma* in the late fifties, but in the end Wyler is not a director one loves so much as tips one's hat to out of respect. I enclose a photocopy of the Wyler entry from my film encyclopedia, which gives a chronology of all his films as well as some interesting bits of information, in particular the fact that in his first two years as a director, he made more than forty two-reel Westerns. There were no film schools back then, but what better school than the intensity of that on-the-job training? Young directors today are not given a chance to fail, to improve steadily from one film to the next. A single flop, and they're out.

Also enclosed: a Xerox of a photograph taken of me at age five in my football uniform. I stumbled across it by accident yesterday—looking through a box for something else—and remembered having written to you about that uniform in an earlier letter. Note how pristine the uniform is. Never touched by a blade of grass or a thimbleful of dirt. And how serious the expression on my face. I wonder who on earth that little boy was.

    With warmest best,

    Paul

P.S.: I have signed up for two of the university roundtables in Canada next September. My first academic conference ever. No, I don't blame you. Anything for a friend.

April 7, 2011

Dear Paul,

Thanks for the observations, and material, on William Wyler. Have you seen *The Children's Hour* (1962), based on a play by Lillian Hellman? I saw it recently for the first time—I mentioned it in my last letter—and thought it a brave film. Or, to be more precise, I thought it brave of Wyler to push a film like that past the gatekeepers of Hollywood. (It would have been even braver, I suppose, to have made it in the 1950s.)

There is a supernumerary pleasure in watching restored black-and-white prints of films that one saw in one's youth (or even in one's childhood) in crummy cinemas with indifferent projectionists and poor projectors. It is only very rarely in color films that one sees black used with all the tonal gradations that it is capable of. It's sad to think there is no audience for new b+w movies.

Is your newly acquired Olivetti one of those little flat jobs that comes in a zip-up canvas carry case? My wife brought one of them to our marriage as part of her dowry. I typed my MA thesis on it. Then in 1972 I bought myself an Adler, a Swiss machine, too heavy to be portable, and used that until computers and printers came along. I won't ever go back to them, the Olivetti and the Adler, but I feel nostalgic about them. I still have them in a cupboard somewhere. God knows where one would buy ribbons nowadays, to say nothing of carbon paper.

You say that you are quite prepared to write novels in which people go around with personal electronic devices. I must say I am not. The telephone is about as far as I will go in a book,

Paul Auster and J. M. Coetzee

and then reluctantly. Why? Not only because I'm not fond of what the world has turned into, but because if people ("characters") are continually going to be speaking to one another at a distance, then a whole gamut of interpersonal signs and signals, verbal and nonverbal, voluntary and involuntary, has to be given up. Dialogue, in the full sense of the term, just isn't possible over the phone.

It had never occurred to me that there is no directory publicly available of people's cell phone numbers. Entrusting someone with one's number has today acquired quite a weight of meaning.

Think of all those old noir movies in which the detective uses the telephone directory to track down his quarry. Cut to close-up of a page in the directory, with a name and number circled in black.

April 18

I've been sleeping badly for years now. I count myself lucky if I can get four hours a night; as for four consecutive hours, that's my idea of bliss.

One consequence is that I nod off during the day, sometimes sitting at my desk—little fugues from the world that usually last no more than a few seconds but sometimes extend to five or even ten minutes.

I've taken to having the most interesting dreams during these escapes: episodes with believable little plots, acutely realistic in their situations, their dialogue, the look of things. They don't seem to be based on memories at all, but to be pure invention. Nothing fantastic in them, nothing menacing. I think of them as finger exercises of the imagination, the improvisations of a mind with something like forty years of practice in conceiving situations. They are of no use to me—they don't fit into what I am writing—so there is no point in noting them down. I am pleased with them, I even enjoy them while they are running, but they leave a residue of sadness too. It seems a pity to have built up, over the decades, this particular little skill, and to think that it is going to be lost, eclipsed, when I go. Not something one can bequeath.

All the best,

John

Paul Auster and J. M. Coetzee

Dear John,

You will have received my little note by now telling you that Siri and I are taking off for Europe again and won't be home until May 30. How good to receive your latest, then— just in the nick of time.

To begin with a last word about William Wyler. In fact, he did make an earlier version of *The Children's Hour*—as long ago as 1936. That adaptation bore the title *These Three*. I saw it at some point in the distant past but can remember nothing about it now except that I thought it was good. (A brief description enclosed, from a video guide we sometimes refer to while watching films.) I will try to track it down after I return. If you happen to find it before then, let me know what you think. It would be interesting to see how the two versions compare with each other.

I don't want to meddle in your private business, but what you report about your sleep problems disturbs me. If I were in your position, I would surely go half mad. What about pills, or a sleep clinic, or some other remedy? One simply cannot survive in a state of permanent exhaustion. It occurs to me that it might have something to do with traveling, your frequent trips to Europe, and the wrenching discombobulation of trying to cope with shifting time zones—especially because you live in Australia, which is devilishly far from everything. Did you have this problem while you were still living in South Africa, or did it begin only after the move? I mentioned your struggles to Siri—because of her deep affection for you, but also because she has studied and written about sleep and knows far more about it than I do—and she was alarmed. She said she wanted to write to you and offer some suggestions. Would that be okay?

On the other hand, the little dreams you talk about are fascinating, and, I think, highly unusual. Most people when they drift off tend to go into a realm of half waking/half sleep in which one encounters a free-for-all of wild, Technicolor images. Your little stories seem to be in black-and-white (that same black-and-white we both miss in contemporary movies), and the fact that they are neither grotesque nor frightening makes them poignant to me. It seems a pity to let this talent go to waste—this unique talent—and even if you feel you can't "use" these dream stories in the work you are doing now, perhaps a day will come when you can approach this phenomenon directly in a work of fiction, an essay, or, even better, a film. I for one would watch (or read) with rapt attention.

A couple of days ago, I had a startling revelation about the effect our correspondence has had on me. We have been at it for close to three years now, and in that time you have become what I would call an "absent other," a kind of adult cousin to the imaginary friends little children invent for themselves. I discovered that I often walk around talking to you in my head, wishing you were with me so I could point out the strange-looking person who just walked past me on the sidewalk, remark on the odd scrap of conversation I just overheard, or take you into the little sandwich shop where I often buy my lunch so you could listen to the talk that goes on in there with me. I love that place, a wholly unpretentious nothing of a place, with its heterogeneous clientele of cops and firemen, hospital workers from across the street, mothers with their children, students, truck drivers, secretaries, and what makes the place

Paul Auster and J. M. Coetzee

special is the men who work behind the counter, good-spirited young guys with their proletarian Brooklyn voices, who seem to know everyone who comes in there ("I talked to your mother yesterday," "I hear your son is doing well on his Little League team," "Welcome back. How was your trip?"), as if I were living in a small provincial town and not in a gigantic metropolis, and I know you would appreciate the spirit inside that shop and understand (if you don't already) what I find so interesting about living in New York. So there you are, John, inside my head as I talk to you, and nothing like this has ever happened to me—probably because I have never corresponded with anyone so regularly—and the effect, I can assure you, is an entirely pleasant one.

A phrase has been running through my head these past few weeks: New Hope for the Dead. It's the title of a pulp novel I read many years ago (a good one, by an American named Charles Willeford), and it sprang to the forefront of my consciousness after reading that Doctorow had just published a new book of short stories at eighty, talking to Coover (seventy-nine) about the Beckett Address he will be delivering in Ireland this fall, having dinner with Roth (seventy-eight) and DeLillo (seventy-four) and finding all of these so-called old men in remarkably good form, busy with projects, cracking jokes, eating with healthy appetites, and I felt encouraged by what I saw and heard. New Hope for the Dead. Meaning: New Hope for Us.

> Until my return. With best thoughts,
>
> Paul

P.S.: Yes, the Olivetti is exactly as you remember it. A little flat job with a zip-up canvas carry case—in this case, a blue case with a black stripe down the middle.

Paul Auster and J. M. Coetzee

Dear John,

I am writing to you from Italy with my new-old Italian typewriter, sitting on the top-floor terrace of the castle where Siri and I have been staying for the past week and looking out at an extraordinarily beautiful landscape of vineyards and hills. What did we do to deserve this? The organizers of the little festival we will be participating in on Friday and Saturday offered us this respite, which we blindly accepted, not knowing what we were getting ourselves into, and everything has turned out better, far better, than we possibly could have imagined. We are the only guests in the hotel, which is indeed a castle, albeit a new one for these parts (circa 1880), an architectural folly that is nevertheless a genuine faux castle, and after three weeks of tramping through cities in northern Europe, the quiet of this place (Novello, in the Langhe hills of Piedmont) has given us a welcome stretch of blissful, unprecedented repose. No obligations, no cares. We write, read, and eat, and every day there is the sun—each day more balmy and sun filled than the day before it.

We began with ten days in Paris, where I had nothing to do but work on my book and see old friends, whereas Siri was inordinately busy with journalists (her novel is just out in France) and various public events. I have watched her address the Paris Society of Psychoanalysts, conduct a contentious, wholly invigorating seminar on trauma and writing at the Sorbonne (at one point, she rolled up her sleeves and said: "I love fighting about ideas"), do an onstage conversation at the Bibliothèque Nationale, take part in a dialogue at Shakespeare and Company with another woman writer that was billed as: "I don't read fiction, but my wife does. Would you dedicate the book to her?," and finally, a double, bilingual reading with the actress Marthe Keller. Then on to Vienna, where she read her much anticipated Sigmund Freud Lecture to a full house. A splendid talk, a brilliant talk, the product of two or three months of brain-splitting work, and there I was sitting in the audience with tears welling up in my eyes as the applause rained down on her. Then we went off in opposite directions for four days, Siri to Germany for readings in Berlin, Hamburg, and Heidelberg, and I to Stockholm, where I began to sing for my supper as well. We joined forces in Copenhagen after that, having promised our Danish publisher to show up for a festival he had organized, our struggling Danish publisher whose company is hanging by a thread, hoping our presence there would give him a boost, and for five days we worked hard, too hard, and by the end we were both dropping from exhaustion. I tallied up Siri's public appearances: fourteen events in nineteen days—an inhuman schedule, which I have made her promise never to repeat for the rest of her life.

Strangely, I seem to have finished my book. After crashing into a wall last November with the novel I had been trying to write (which I told you about earlier), I took a pause, and a couple of days into the new year began writing something else: an autobiographical work, a collection of fragments and memories, a curious project that revolves around the history of my body, the physical self I have been dragging around with me for sixty-four years now. Two hundred pages later, I feel that I have said enough, and after Siri read through it yesterday and gave it the stamp of approval, I suddenly find myself unemployed again. That is why I am writing this extra letter to you—because I am living in a faux castle in Italy and don't know what to do with myself today. Another letter, then, in order to fill these tranquil morning hours and share two little anecdotes with you, two sentences that have been ringing in my head for some time.

1. "They all think it's never going to end."

Every September, a festival of American films is held in Deauville, France—the new films that will be appearing in both countries that fall. I don't know how or why the festival was started, but every year an award is given (or used to be given) to an American writer for the body of his work. In 1994, I turned out to be that lucky man, and when I was told that Mailer and Styron had both won in previous years, I decided it was an honor worth crossing the Atlantic for, so off Siri and I went to the Normandy resort town of Deauville. It was a good year to be there—the fiftieth anniversary of the D-day landings. To mark the occasion, the festival had invited various children and grandchildren of the Allied generals, among them one of Leclerc's descendants and Eisenhower's grand-daughter, Susan. Siri and I wound up spending some time with Susan Eisenhower (we liked her very much), and when we found out that she was a "Russia expert" who was married to a scientist from one of the republics of the former Soviet Union, we both understood that the cold war was indeed over. Eisenhower's granddaughter married to a Soviet scientist!

Also to mark the occasion, the festival had scheduled screenings of films about World War II and had sent out invitations to some of the old American actors who had appeared in them. That was how we got to meet such people as Van Johnson (deaf as a post), Maureen O'Hara (still beautiful), and Roddy McDowall. At one point during the dinner we attended with those bygone movie stars, O'Hara leaned over to McDowall and asked: "Roddy, how long have we known each other?" To which McDowall replied: "Fifty-four years, Maureen." They had acted together in John Ford's *How Green Was My Valley*. Astonishing to have been there, to have witnessed that exchange.

One of the other people who came that year was Budd Schulberg. I had met him a couple of times in America, and his connection to Hollywood films probably went further into the past than anyone else in the land of the living, since his father had been B. P. Schulberg, the head of Paramount in the twenties and thirties, and all the way back when he was nineteen years old, Budd had collaborated on a screenplay with F. Scott Fitzgerald. The man who wrote *On the Waterfront*, author of one of the best novels about Hollywood, *What Makes Sammy Run?*, as well as the script of Bogart's last film, *The Harder They Fall*, an excellent movie set in the world of boxing—a complex man, a former Communist Party member who had named names before HUAC in the late forties or early fifties, but from what I have read, he turned against the party with great violence after they tried to interfere with his work and condemned them as bastards one and all. Anyway, I didn't know him well, we were causal acquaintances at best, but I had enjoyed talking to him back in America, always struck by how well he spoke in spite of a double speech impediment (stutter and lisp), and now, at Deauville in 1994, we unexpectedly ran into each other in the lobby of the hotel where we were both staying, where everyone involved with the festival was staying (movie stars, directors, producers, young actors and actresses), and because we were both waiting for our wives to come downstairs for dinner, we sat down together on a bench in the lobby and quietly surveyed the hectic comings and goings of the rich and famous and beautiful. In rushed Tom Hanks (it was the year of *Forrest Gump*—a dreadful film in case you are tempted to see it), in rushed a glamorous starlet with her entourage, in rushed numerous others, all of them looking confident, filled with a sense of their own importance, *on top of the world*, as if each one of them in fact *owned the world*, and after a while Budd turned to me, the eighty-year-old Budd, who had been watching such people since he was a child, who had been at the top and been at the bottom, the wise old man who both stuttered and lisped turned to me and said: "They all think it's never going to end."

2. "They were all dead."

The third Hustvedt sister is married to a sculptor named Jon Kessler, and for twenty-five years Jon and I have been good friends—brothers-in-law who treat each other more as brothers than as in-laws. Jon's great-uncle, Bernie Kamber, who died a few years ago in his early nineties, was a marvelous character who worked as a press agent for Hollywood films in the forties, fifties, and sixties, a throwback figure to the time of Damon Runyon, who spoke a particular form of New Yorkese that has now vanished from the face of the earth and who, in his dotage, liked nothing better than to share stories with us about his youthful escapades. He seemed to have known everyone, from Rita Hayworth to Joe DiMaggio and Marilyn Monroe, George Burns (who was his closest friend), and especially Burt Lancaster, for whom he worked on several projects. "Burt was a serious guy," he told us once, "and he read a lot of heavy books. You know, people like Pluto and Aristotle." (Pluto—the cartoon dog—not Plato.) One of my favorite Bernie stories goes back to the war, when the U.S. and the Soviet Union were allies. He was responsible for promoting a mediocre film called *Three Russian Girls*, and for the opening night in Kansas City he had come up with a plan to draw a large crowd to the theater: anyone willing to donate a pint of blood to our Russian friends would be let in for free. As Bernie told it, he got to the theater a bit late, after the film had started, and as he approached the entrance, he saw the theater owner standing on the sidewalk engaged in a loud argument with a man. Bernie asked what was wrong, and the exasperated owner wailed: "You and your big ideas. This guy wants his blood back!"

Such was Jon's Uncle Bernie. One evening a couple of years before he died, Bernie told us that he had been reading a new biography of John F. Kennedy. In the book, he was both happy and surprised to stumble across some references to a well-known brothel from the 1950s, a place that Kennedy had apparently frequented and which Bernie and many of his friends were also familiar with. Excited to share these passages with his old pals, Bernie went to the phone to ring them up, but as he went down the list in his mind, he understood that none of them was in a position to answer his call. "They were all dead," he told us. Bernie had outlived his friends, and now that he was the last man standing, there was no one left for him to talk to about the past. He made me think of one of those anthropological oddities I have occasionally read about: the last living member of his tribe, the last person to speak a language—which will become extinct upon his death.

Warmest greetings from Neverland,

Paul

Dear Paul,

Thanks for the letter of April 22. I hope your European trip is going well.

You write of me as the "absent other" to whom you find yourself talking in your head. Let me make a parallel but somewhat different admission. I have been to your home but, as you know, have not seen the apartment—rather simply appointed, as you describe it—in which you work. Now and again I have visions of you in this apartment, which in my imagination is painted white, well lit, and windowless, not unlike one of your fictional spaces of confinement. You sit at your desk, your fingers poised over your typewriter, which in these visions is a rather ancient, bulky Remington (sometimes the ribbon sticks and you have to release it: the black smudge on your thumb is by now ingrained). There you sit, hour after hour, day after day, wrapped in your thoughts.

Seeing you thus, I feel a certain fraternal tenderness for you and your dogged, unappreciated bravery. Of course I know there is another, public face you wear—that of the admired man of letters. But I am convinced my vision of you as voluntary prisoner of the Muse is more true. The world is at his feet, I think to myself, yet there he is at eight-thirty every morning, unlocking the door of his cell, checking in for the new day's punishment.

I know there is a lot of romantic bullshit spoken about the writing life, about the despair of confronting the blank page, about the anguish of inspiration that won't come, about unpredictable—and unreliable—fits of sleepless, fevered creation, about the nagging and unquenchable self-doubt, and so on.

But it's not entirely bullshit, is it? Writing is a matter of giving and giving and giving, without much respite. I think of the pelican that Shakespeare is so fond of, that tears open its breast in order to feed its offspring on its blood (what a bizarre piece of folklore!). So I think of you in that lonely place, dishing up yourself into the gaping mouth of the Remington.

I confess I have some minor difficulty fitting the sandwich shop you describe into this picture of monastic privation. But then I think, maybe when Paul visits the sandwich shop he sits in a corner, silent and unrecognized, and slips away like a ghost as soon as he has eaten.

New Hope for the Dead: that's a great title. What a pity it's already taken.

Thanks for your kind concern over my insomnia. I hesitate to authorize you to ask Siri to write, not because I don't believe she has specialized knowledge but because I feel I am beyond help. I had a long series of meetings with a sleep specialist a couple of years ago. She was pretty up-to-date, I thought, and prescribed a regimen for me which might have worked had I lived a more regular life and been a tougher character. But in the end I just couldn't face the misery of forced rising at 3:00 A.M. followed by battling to stay awake through the day until a 9:00 or 10:00 P.M. bedtime. And anyway—as the therapist was forced to acknowledge—any gains I made were lost as soon as I traveled abroad across time zones, and subverted a second time when I returned.

Curiously, I find it easier to sleep in Western Europe, which happens to share a time zone with my natal South Africa, than in Australia. Perhaps, even after nine years, my organism has not adjusted to the Antipodes.

Thank you for the long and happy-sounding letter from your Italian castle (May 24). What did you do to deserve such good fortune?, you ask. The answer: this particular episode of good fortune makes up for an equivalent episode of bad fortune that hit you sometime in the past, an episode you have forgotten about because it is not your manner to hold grudges against fate.

So you have completed a two-hundred-page history of your body. What an interesting idea, and how I envy you for not only having the idea but also giving it flesh—always the more difficult part. I'll wait to see whether you deal with your body part by part or treat it integrally.

I've always found it interesting that whereas we human beings think of our bodies as having parts—arms, legs, and so forth—animals don't. In fact, I doubt that animals think of themselves as "having" bodies at all. They just are their bodies.

I'll be attending a conference on Samuel Beckett in the UK next month. Foolishly, I consented to do an e-mail interview with one of the organizers beforehand, on the subject of my relations with Beckett. As he and I are discovering, I don't have anything new to say about Beckett, and perhaps don't even have a relation with him. I certainly wouldn't be the kind of writer I am if Beckett had never been born, but that sort of debt—call it a debt, for want of a better word—is best not scrutinized. I'd rather simply pay my silent respects at the SB shrine or the SB temple (I've never visited the SB gravestone).

All the best,

John

June 14, 2011

Dear John,

So good to hear from you.

Just to put your mind at rest: I don't eat lunch in the sandwich shop. On most mornings, I go there on my way to work and order something to take out—which I eat several hours later in my little apartment, always in utmost solitude. I am in the shop for approximately four to seven minutes, and except for telling the counterman what kind of sandwich I want, I rarely say anything to anyone. But how much one can see and hear in four to seven minutes!

They know me there, however (at least a couple of the workers do), since I mentioned the place by name in *The Brooklyn Follies* and stole a remark made to Siri by one of the countermen about ten years ago. From the book: "I was intending to ask for a cinnamon-raisin bagel, but the word caught in my mouth and came out as *cinnamon-reagan.* Without missing a beat, the young guy behind the counter answered: 'Sorry, we don't have any of those. How about a pumpernixon instead?'"

The work space actually has several windows and a good deal of light. The typewriter is not a Remington but an Olympia—but no matter, the ink smudges my thumbs every time I put in a new ribbon, and the spirit of the place—if not the physical environment—is very much as you imagine it. And no, what you say is not entirely bullshit, and I am touched, in fact deeply touched, that you understand me well enough by now to know that the most significant part of my life takes place within the silence of those four walls. The word "bravery" might be a bit excessive (I have never thought of myself as brave), but that doesn't mean I don't appreciate the thought.

I have continued to worry about your sleep problems, and now that I have been back for two weeks and am still struggling to readjust to New York time (waking at five every morning), I am convinced that what you are suffering from is a prolonged case of jet lag—a nine-year case of jet lag, the worst case of jet lag in recorded history. The only way to cure it would be to stop traveling for a year or two, to stay put in Australia and let your body finally adapt itself to the demands of living in that far-flung place. But now you are off to a Beckett conference in England! (Nearly every time we write to each other, it seems that one of us is about to take off for another country.) If you can't control your impulse to travel to Europe several times a year, then perhaps the answer (dare I say it? it seems so simple and obvious) is to pull up stakes again and move to Europe. A logical solution, perhaps—but then again, life is not logical, and you must live where you feel happiest. On the other hand: you must sleep. You absolutely must sleep.

As for the new book about my body—no, it is not an anatomical breakdown of one piece of me after the other. There are disquisitions on pleasures and pains (sex and food, for example, as well as illnesses and broken bones), some long passages about my mother (in whose body my own body began), a list of all the places where I have ever lived (the domiciles in which my body has been sheltered), reflections on deformity, death, and experiences that could have led to death but didn't . . .

Thinking about the book, it suddenly occurs to me that it might be a good idea to read from it when we do our joint event in Canada this September. And no sooner do I mention Canada than I think about Portugal in November. I just had breakfast with Paulo Branco—who is in New York for a couple of days—and he said he is going to send you a formal invitation to be on the jury again. Because of the financial crisis in Portugal, there was some question about whether the festival would be held this year, but Paulo assures me that the problems have been solved and all is well. I am going, Siri is going, our daughter Sophie is going (to sing), and I hope that you and Dorothy will be going as well. A pox on jet lag! How good it will be to spend some time with you there.

Another chapter from the ongoing saga of *New Hope for the Dead*:

My first wife's mother lived to be a hundred, perhaps even a hundred and one. Born in 1903, the youngest of six or seven children, she once showed me a photograph taken before her first birthday, a family portrait that included her parents, her siblings, her aunts and uncles, her cousins, her grandparents, and herself, a small baby sitting on someone's lap. Standing to the far left in the back row was an old man with a white beard. She told me he was her great-uncle and that he was ninety-nine years old when the picture was taken. I quickly did the math in my head and realized that he had been born in 1805. *Four years before Abraham Lincoln.* It was 1967 when I held that picture in my hand, and I still remember the overpowering effect it had on me. I said to myself: "I am talking to a person who knew someone who was born before Abraham

Lincoln." One hundred and sixty-two years: the blink of an eye! Now, forty-four years later, I say to myself: Two hundred and six years—the blink of an eye!

As ever,

Paul

Paul Auster and J. M. Coetzee

Dear Paul,

I recently came across a posthumously published poem by A. R. Ammons: Getting old gets old, he says; even trying to find something new to say about getting old gets old. I don't feel that way at all, though I am nearly as old as Ammons was when he wrote the poem. Things keep being revealed to me, or at least coming into sharper focus. What I see, I see more clearly than when I was young. Am I deluded?

For instance Libya. Who would have thought that our attention would, for a space, be fixed on events in this neglected corner of the world! And how good it is for one's general sense of things to behold one of the world's nastier dictators being brushed away. It is almost as though the gods have organized a piece of theater for our benefit, to reassure us that there is, after all, justice in the universe, that if only we will wait long enough the wheel of fortune will turn and the high and mighty be brought level with the earth.

Of course (here enters the spirit of Ammonian pessimism) the euphoria in the streets of Tripoli, like the euphoria in the streets of Cairo, will die down as the reality of unpaid salaries, power cuts, and uncollected garbage hits home; and doubtless the regime that replaces Gaddafi will turn out to be venal and corrupt and perhaps even dictatorial too. But at least those young men careering around in their Toyota pickups, firing their Kalashnikovs in the air, will have something to remember for the rest of their lives, something to tell the grandchildren. Glory days! Perhaps that is what revolutions are really about, perhaps that is all one should expect from them: a week or two of freedom, of exulting in one's strength and beauty (and of being loved by all the girls), before the gray old men reassert their grip and life is returned to normal.

The world keeps throwing up its surprises. We keep learning.

Yours fraternally,

John

Paul Auster and J. M. Coetzee

www.vintage-books.co.uk